# Life On, In And Along The Thames

To Roxanne & Bob —

Good friends are hard to find —— Enjoy —

Dan E Blackstone

# Life On, In And Along The Thames

## 1930'S TO EARLY 1940'S

Dan E. Blackstone

**To order additional copies of this book, contact:**
Xlibris LLC
1-888-795-4274
www.Xlibris.com
Orders@Xlibris.com
137445

# Contents

# ACKNOWLEDGEMENTS

$W$e had an adventurous life, exposures to a multitude of activities that others can only dream about. Almost on a daily basis I am reminded by someone who unwittingly says or imitates an act that causes a recall of our childhood. Thank you.

The book would not be complete without acknowledging the neighbors and friends we knew. Some of them are . . . .

From Laurel Hill: Dudu S, Johnny S, Popeye, Lucille, Skippy, Big Fool, Boof maker, Beans, Hop-a-long, 4 eyes, Shrimp, Malc, Potts, Charlie P, Jack Allen, Joey & Eddie S, Joey S, Charlie & Ralph N., Doc Jensen, Walker twins, Edjew—Edgew?, Al D, Erickson, Herrick, James & j? twins, Robert J, Marvin J, Marshall & Murray, Bobby & Tony W., Bobby N, Bobby H, Elwood B, Evelyn F, Evelyn G, Harriet, Jean, Gloria, Louise, Stephanie, Frannie, Alice, Lisha, Ruth, Laura, Dottie S, Lorraine, Virginia (Eliz)?

On Rogers Ave, Crowe, Rogers, and Hoelck.
On Sunnyside, Clay, etc. a "raft" of people . . .

Some fine teachers from NFA: Mr. de Courcy, Miss Peck, Miss McMann, Miss Pryor (sp), Miss Cupit, Miss Triplett, Mrs. Browning
Grade school teachers: Miss Adams, Miss Kilroy, Miss Cloon (sp), Miss Driscoll

And from the "Bums" (Thamesville side): Barbara L, Shirley and Edith A., Cavete (sp), Donald B, Rosalie C, Hayes Brothers, June and Russell B,

And others I can't recall.

In the book I refer to an apple tree, different coves, calm waters, stone walls and young people. I mention a few people who have been influential in my life, so I have included several short pieces that represent the influence of these people and places.

All errors and misspellings are mine and mine alone.

Special thanks to author, Nancy Rustici, for suggestions and directions, to an unknown English teacher at the time, who repeatedly told me to write by the name of Wally Lamb, and to Jean Blackstone, without whose computer skills I'd never have completed this missile, and of course, Barbara Aiello, a steadfast encourager, a source of comfort, a real nice lady.

dan

1. Hollyhock Island
2. Coal Dock
3. Broadway School
4. RR Tunnel
5. Gas Plant
6. RR Bridge East Side
7. East Side
8. Switch Yard
9. Lumber & Dahl Oil
10. Fill Area of Old Cove
11. Cove
12. Blueberry Lots
13. Dock & Swim Area
14. Thermos Co.
15. Rope Swing
16. Apple Tree
17. Fish Trapping Area
18. Water Tank—RR
19. State Hospital
20. Draw Bridge
21. Trading Cove RR Bridge
22. Thames River Pirates
23. Woolen Mill
24. Thamesville Bums

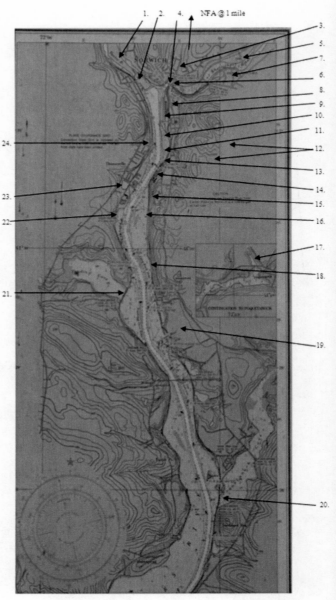

# CHAPTER I

## THE RIVER

Adventure . . . Imagination . . . Visions past, present and future . . . If the river could speak, what grand accolades it could bestow upon those who were a part of Her. Yes, Her, for she mothered many in their childhood quest for education, success and just searching for the unknown. What a learning experience. What opportunities! She provided that rampantly enhanced creativity of untold champions victorious in every adventure. Only the river knows, what we, the youth who lived along her banks, learned from Her and the comfort we found as we dove into her welcoming arms.

At first, she was a fearsome obstacle; a body with no regard for lives or recognition of the uninitiated. Gradually we came to know a more loving, kinder river, ever giving and protector to those who understood and appreciated her. No one group knew more of her various moods than we who interacted with Her daily and ventured out upon her surface even in the most tempestuous conditions, even in a hurricane! We all loved that river unconditionally. Actually, she romanced us. The so called "Bums" and "Rats" (us) enjoyed her enticing invitations to communicate with her in every possible and thinkable manner. Once we learned her language, there was no stopping our adventures with her and through her.

The starting point in telling this tale must be the first time we saw Her. We were not born near Her, the river that is. Our nurturing began when we moved from a farm environment to the city at ages eight and nine. Along her magnificent flowing eddies created by breakwaters, points of land, jetties, docks, sand bars and mud flats, we learned Her ways. The barriers were resistant to the changing tides, causing entirely different swirls depending on whether it was a flood or ebb tide, with or without wind, or the river's own direction. Our first view inspired awe; young and impressionable and a little intimidated especially when our parents instructed us to stay away from Her, because they feared we'd be swept away. Probably that was the concern of every parent, since we only lived a few hundred feet from its bank, although we were sixty to eighty feet above Her. After that *view from above*, Her allure drew us to seek a way to reach Her.

By walking across the street we came to a sidewalk, a fence three to four feet in height and then a wall that went down twenty to twenty five feet to a garden. It was well kept and practically weed free. About two hundred feet to the left there was a small dirt road, with a cobble stone monument with a perfectly round stone sphere on top of it. Crown Hill led to several houses, circled round to the left, passed an opening on the right that led to the river. A path to the river had been found! The road continued up around the gas storage sphere back to the main road which was next to the school.

Eventually we found a second route between two houses across the street, which was the shortest way to the river. A dirt path snaked back and forth down a sixty + degree slope past 'Jimmy-the-beggar's' house to the tracks. Besides the switch-backs, there was one other way that was used periodically. Near Frannie's porch was a tree that we used, but being so close to her house and knowing Frannie's parents were not too fond of anyone using that method of descent, we rarely used it. My brother reminded me that we had a small tree growing near our second floor bedroom window, and once I tried to use it as an escape route only to have it snap off so that I landed in a heap with the tree.

Railroad tracks ran along on both sides of the river; another obstacle to overcome in our quest to reach the river. Parental fear about the safety of their children was overcome within a short time frame and we were allowed to cross over the tracks to see kids fishing and setting eel-pots and minnow pots. After all, ALL the other kids were doing it!

The river was still a challenge. We hadn't been on Her or over Her or in Her, only to the edge near the small rickety docks, some of which were so wobbly only three or four people at most could stand on them at one time. The cove at perigee, the lowest of tides, had only a few inches of water covering the mud and sand in places. That fact was discovered once when we attempted to wade out: the mud was at least a foot in depth, or so it seemed. Disaster! A well planned trip out to the breakwater was spoiled due to blackish brown mire. Eventually we discovered there was a way to walk out to the end of the breakwater without having to go over a quarter of a mile out of the way; then a quarter mile to the end of the breakwater, instead of travelling only two hundred to three hundred feet from the docks, thereby saving close to a mile walk out and back. When we first moved, we were restricted to the back woods and an occasional excursion to the river. Each time we became more enthralled and Her call became clearer and louder. Once everyone learned to swim, the restrictions were lifted by the parents and by the next summer we had unlimited access, as long as we mentioned where we were going.

During the winter we had walked along her banks for miles in each direction becoming familiar with her coves, feeders, and islands that we could see from the shore. It was tempting to walk on the ice to the islands. There was a glaze on the rocks of the breakwaters at first and chunks of ice standing upright on the edge at low tides. It was too dangerous to walk on the breakwater and the ice was different thicknesses due to freezing at different times. The ice blocks were on such steep angles along the breakwaters that it was impossible to attempt crossing to the islands. We learned early that it was dangerous to walk on thin ice because the water beneath it would still run and should you fall in, you probably would not make it back to the surface. The water would carry you down stream under the ice where you could become trapped. We considered kicking the ice rather than trying to break it with our hands. But eventually it was decided these ideas wouldn't work. The best survival technique was to throw out your arms to each side to keep you from going under.

Breakwater with ice in cove

Thinking back about the blocks of ice, there was a stupid thing we did. The river would occasionally freeze so that it was possible to cross to the other side and back. Sometimes it would stay frozen for over a week, and that is when we saw our first ice breakers. These ships would come up the channel to open it so that boat traffic could pass, delivering coal and oil to the storage areas, as well as some other commodities. The ice breakers would ride up river and break the ice, which in some cases was as much as twelve inches thick. With the clearing of the channel our river crossing days were over, but we'd travel out to the breakwater and walk downstream at the ice edge to the navigation light past the dock. In the summer it was expected that your shoes (Keds) would get wet, but in the winter it meant detailed explanations to our parents, which we wished to avoid, so we would build a fire and dry our clothes, shoes and socks but especially our shoes. Once when we were trying to cross the river, it was starting to breakup and we hopped from one block of ice to the next block of ice. We made it until we got close to our home shore at the red beacon light, which was where the deepest water was and also the steepest part of the shore line. The stream was swift there as it turned back to the main channel. When the ice floe was only about three feet from the shore we decided to jump. Under normal circumstances that would have been a regular activity, but our feet were wet, the ice floe was wet, and it was moving. In preparation for the leap, the ice floe tilted, but the leap was made! Well, almost. As our feet pushed off from the ice floe, it went in the opposite direction hence we landed in thigh deep water a foot from the shore. You guessed correctly if you said wet feet, wet clothes and what made it worse, there was no time to build a fire, for it was time to be home.

'YOU DID WHAT?' Never do that again! Of course, we didn't try that again. Well, Renfrew of the Mounted did it, why not us? No dice. He was trained, we were not.

The reason we didn't always try to get onto the ice

The islands we mentioned, we were sure were possible locations for Captain Kidd's treasures or maybe some treasures from some other long forgotten adventurer. With each sighting our imaginations would be stimulated to the point that we would actually make notes to remind ourselves which island or cove should be visited if we ever got a boat. We especially loved the large cove across the river even though there was a larger cove called the Draw-Bridge Cove on our side (Poquetanuck). That was close to four miles downstream. It never seemed quite as inviting as the one across the river.

Across the river there was another group of dare-devils similar to us. Some of them were about the same age, and several were a few years older, making them more experienced and without question, more knowledgeable in the ways of the world. During the 1930's if you could find enough money to buy bugler, a soda, a devil-dog, or a grinder you were considered a wonder. That crew always seemed to have unlimited supplies.

It was about that time that we learned about smoking, hence the reference to Bugler which is tobacco in a paper pouch. You had to roll your own, unless you had access to a rolling machine. One of our pastimes was to ask if storekeepers had 'Prince Albert' in the can. They'd say yes and the kids would say, 'Why don't you let him out?' Yes, we indulged in smoking. Even though it was not a real pleasant experience, in order to look good in the eyes of the rest of the gang we never let on how dizzy we were or that we were on the verge of regurgitating. Swallow that saliva . . . Inhale . . . but not deeply because you learned very quickly to fake the inhalation part so as not to feel ill. No matter, eventually we all became smokers. Really dumb, but in order to fit in, we succumbed. Eventually, most of us gave it up especially after serving in the military. That was a long time and in some cases, too late. One of the competitions in which we engaged during our smoking at the dock side, was to expectorate, a new word we learned and overly verbalized in the beginning. That was so you didn't have to swallow the tobacco-laden saliva! Yeah, I know, spitting is the word we used also, but it developed into quite a sport. Some of the guys eventually went in for tobacco chewing and became quite accurate in spitting and attained great distances easily measured by the splash in the river.

I must digress at this point to mention that smoking was not approved by many parents. When we got caught, our father just sat us down and had a smoke with us, only he gave us both, my brother and me, a cigar. It was a White Owl, a popular brand that cost a nickel apiece! I sat at the kitchen table and so did 'Pop'. My brother stood and actually walked around the kitchen while smoking. I wanted to get up and spit, but Pop said no, swallow. A real smoker swallows his saliva, sick! There is no way I can express how I felt. I wanted to get up and get rid of the cigar, but NO! I had to finish it! His comment was 'Look at your brother, he is over half way through his. And he was. But what Pop didn't know was that my brother had broken off over half of the cigar, so he actually smoked less than half. No need to finish the story, I was sick, and eventually vomited. You'd think that we'd learn, especially after being told it would stunt our growth but we went back to smoking had bait, and crab nets. Someone found out about spot-lighting and scooping! It was then we needed a flashlight, and preferably a boat, but until that time, we walked along the shore and climbed over rocks to scoop the blue crabs that were visible in the light. One held the light, the other the dip-net. Another way of getting crabs was to watch to see if any old carcasses were in the water; they always attracted the crabs. Occasionally someone would drop a burlap bag into the area and the crabs would suddenly appear at that location in a short time. Pulling the bag out revealed that someone had sunk some kittens or puppies that were unwanted. It was then that we learned about the one brick, two brick, three brick method of sinking the lot. We would then make comments about a dog or something being a six brick or eight brick item. It was amazing to see how many unwanted objects we'd find in our area or other more distant areas. We never understood why anyone would sink chickens though.

# CHAPTER II

## SWIMMING AND TRAINS

$O$ne of the statements that was often made by people of our generation had something to do with, "DO YOU HAVE". For example, do you have clean underwear on? 'Why?' 'Suppose something happened, you had an accident?' I often wondered if there was some magical charm about clean underwear that protected you from harm.

There were so many superstitions we were exposed to through friendships with other kids, especially those who were first generation immigrants. Black cats going under ladders, avoiding cracks on the sidewalks, only climbing the left side of trees, carry a stick in your left hand while walking a stone wall, check your fingernails for white spots near the quick, never light three buglers on one match. Of course with that one we tried to stretch it, often with everyone crossing their finger and not telling the others about it but those are just a few. Do you have clean feet before putting on clean socks? The rest of your body could be filthy, but if your feet are clean, then no one will notice the B.O. Back to the underwear, I can recall the winter underwear, long johns with flap, (which had buttons on the upper corners), or sometimes body suits with short sleeves and cut off legs, I think they were called union suits. Some of the spring wear was similar but of very light weight. The underwear of summer was problematical for me! We wore shorts, overalls, (with bibs sometimes, which we hated) or some hand-me-downs and of course, KEDS. (If you wore CONVERSE you were too rich for our group and your mother wouldn't let you play with us! Well, not really.) Looking back on the Keds vs. Converse controversy, I recall that the Converse were faster and you could actually jump higher than anyone else. The reason the Converse always went faster and jumped higher was that all the older boys taking gym had them issued to them by the school if they played on the team. But that didn't last long, we finally figured out the real reason. The other kids were older and more adept at jumping, but it made for interesting challenges and gave us goals for which to strive.

In any event, as I try to recall, wearing undergarments would be a tremendous hindrance or disadvantage to our swimming program. That meant a delay of a few seconds before you could hit the water. Last one in is "it" for our water tag game. You could only tag while you were in the water. The dock, or anything connected to it, was a refuge. Rules changed rather abruptly sometimes, depending on how big you were. We may have gone swimming anywhere between two to eight times a day. At ten seconds delay each time to remove underwear, that was up to eighty seconds per day. To simplify we'll say sixty seconds. That's one whole minute per day. We'd even go swimming on rainy days, so inclement weather would not hinder us. That would be ninety days in the summer alone, but our season would start April first and run to October. For the summer alone, that would mean ninety minutes, or one and a half hour of lost swim time. It was much better not to wear undergarments and gain the time for swimming. 'YOU DID WHAT WITH YOUR UNDERWEAR?'

Swimming was a major activity and everyone learned to swim at a young age as it was either learn to swim or you couldn't be involved in the creative activities along and in the river. Eventually there came a real challenge, the first of many, but the major one, the most crucial was swimming across the river to the docks of our friendly rivals. After a brief pause and congratulatory activity with them, we had to make the return trip. The Bums had an equal challenge to their crew, and would swim over to our side. We never went alone. We had more sense than that. We used logs at first, then we were accompanied by kayaks made by us; they were crooked and malformed but seaworthy. Sure they leaked a little, but we made them out of slim pieces of wood, and green boughs wrapped with old sheets in lieu of canvas. Then they were heavily layered with paint. I have no recollection of where the paint came from. The kayaks worked, and the canvas wrapped 'Viking ships' were the ones that acted as patrol boats. What a thrill to have been over and back at slack tide. After a few trips of that nature, it was time to attempt the next hurdle, of making the trip during an ebbing tide, then half ebbing tide, and before low tide during the swiftest moving water. We learned to compensate for the current and make the line across without being swept too far off course. Mother River was a great teacher. In later years when flying in aircraft I had no problems with drift or yaw or crab when mentioned. I had learned those things at age ten or eleven from the greatest of instructors, the river. Of course, some of the times we'd start across only to return after a few minutes due to the strong sea-breeze coming up river and on occasion down river. This caused a chop and huge wave action, white caps. The down river breeze only bothered us in later years when we had a boat and were several miles downstream. The headwind would be so difficult, that it would necessary to head for shore and pole or pull the boat back to a sheltered area, using a long rope. Someone would stand in the boat holding it off the shore by using an oar as a pole. If we were lucky, we'd get back, otherwise, the boat would be secured and picked up when the wind subsided.

The area in which most of us learned to swim was an old dock where barges once unloaded and where small tankers and ferry boats tied up when it was in vogue to travel to and from other ports via boats before the active use of trains. My mother lived adjacent to the river when she was a very young girl and she and her sisters would lie on the floor of their upstairs landing where there was a full floor length window and they'd watch the ferries go past. Some ferries had side wheels and on one or two occasions it had a rear wheel paddle, but most were the side wheelers (so she said). I suspect that is why my mother was never really worried about us when we were at the river, because she remembered her early experiences. Actually we learned to swim in another location. It was in a canal section leading to a power house. We perfected our swimming at the dock, but I must add that we always went swimming on April first, even in the snow on one occasion.

One of our earlier explorations along the river came with walking the tracks where we picked up coke and coal for the furnace. The old steam engines were periodically getting rid of ashes and in the ash there was coke, sometimes coal. We'd carry it home and try to use it in order to save money for our parents. Actually, it was their directive for us to walk the track looking for this commodity. I suppose I should tell the story that my mother told me. When she lived in the house near the river (and it must have been a magnificent home), her mother would go and pick up coal for the kitchen cook stove. They lived near a trestle and at one end, the train crew would slow to dump ashes. The fireman would stoke the fire and shovel coal into the boiler or firebox and some coal would inadvertently fall off, so my grandmother would walk to that area with a few children after the train passed slowly over the trestle. Once when she was there the train came by while she was picking up the coal, and the fireman saw her, waved to her and threw off several shovels-full of coal for them. This went on for awhile and once during the summer she stood in the middle of the tracks and stopped the train to give the crew vegetables and jars of preserves, telling them that when they saw the flag she had put up on a stool or table, they were to stop and pick up what she had left for them. This continued until the Christmas when our grandparents' house burned on Christmas Eve. I often wondered what would have happened if they had kept leaving vegetables and canned gods for a period of years. I thought of the gumption and courage displayed by our grandmother to stand in the middle of the tracks and stop a train! I also wonder what kind of life we would have had if the house had not burned. All these questions. Too bad, they will go unanswered.

Anyhow, I suspect my mother let us go to the tracks after we had been advised of their dangers. Even though the trains went by on a very strict schedule we were never intimidated by them and the river side was always the side we went to stand when a train came past. We learned to listen for certain sounds that came from the rails which warned us of an approaching train. The river side. The friendly safe feeling of a 'protector'. Our home away from home, especially if we were at the old dock. There was plenty of room there to stand and wave if a passenger train was passing, even though those trains were not that frequent. We never thought about needing a bathing suit on when the trains passed, but once we realized the situation, we would jump into the water when one came along. But shortly after that time we all started using bathing suits, or short pants because passenger trains came more frequently in the early 1940's. The advent of the 'Budd' cars, a single passenger car with a diesel engine that carried defense workers to the Groton ship yards from Massachusetts and Hartford areas occurred around that time.

Another activity that prompted competition among us was introduced. Swimming under water. This new activity was adopted because of our game of tag. The rules, however, changed periodically. Swimming under water was a great escape method. The dock was always a safe haven or refuge so if you kept the participants away from it, you had a chance to tag them. Visibility was limited in the water due to many factors, especially the amount of tannin plus the sediments in suspension. It gave a yellowish-brownish tint to our bodies underwater and visibility was only a few feet until you went deep enough to get past the thermo cline. Beans, a good buddy and one of several Negroes had a beautiful bronze body and would completely disappear almost instantly just a few inches below the surface. At the depth of the thermo-cline, which varied on a daily basis, you'd have much clearer vision of the bottom after passing through it into the colder, denser water. We learned about haloclines, the layers of salt that caused the lines in the water as we passed though to greater depths from fresh water to brackish water to what we discovered later was a salt wedge from the incoming tide. Our tag games were proving grounds for future shocks to coaches at the YMCA ( we would occasionally get invited during the winter to attend church functions or Boy Scout outings there). We surprised the management with our swimming and diving abilities especially our underwater distances, without ever having been coached, My brother was pretty sensational and claimed the best distance for underwater swimming. It became a contest that lasted for many years. We'd practice holding our breaths while walking the rails or running the ties; (three ties was the usual stride). We did a sort of hop to make it, but occasionally we'd up it to four and count while holding our breaths. Three may not seem like much, but it required a slight spring to make it and four required a mini leap. Recalling the record would be futile besides, we'd fudge and add a few seconds or one up one another periodically. Three point five to four minutes comes to mind.

With swimming was the sudden realization that there was a world of diving. That meant we needed a diving board. Our usual walk along the tracks uptown meant a detour through the lumber yard adjacent to the tracks and river, actually between the railroad yard and the river. At one time lumber came by boat, hence the dockage that surrounded the harbor. We'd walk through the yard on a 'spotting' tour. We'd look for old, weathered planks, locate a couple that were not too warped or twisted badly, and set them aside.

After acquiring them, there was the digging of a hole on the land side of the dock, inserting the plank so that it extended out past the dock at a 10 to 15 degree angle, enough to give us a good spring. Large rocks were rolled and placed over the buried part of the plank to hold it in place. The first spring caused the plank to vibrate and continued to slap the dock for a few seconds making a staccato sound after the diver had plummeted head over heels into Mother River. The plank was lashed to the dock with rope so as to prevent this action. Eventually the rope was replaced with wooden or metal strips of some sort. This was quite an engineering feat for those formally unschooled. The diving board gave us the opportunity to learn flips, full and half gainers, jack-knives, swan dive, especially the type Johnny Weissmuller

did off the cliffs or high jungle trees or what-ever, (or was it Buster
Crabbe?) We learned those dives from seeing the ten cent movie
serials. Never would we understand why they always did a swan dive,
taking a chance of injury from such heights but we had to try as well.
In order to attain these heights, we would bounce several times to get
the maximum spring, then reenact what we thought was a replication
of the dives in the movies. It taught us about how our bodies could
be used and catapulted us to fame amongst ourselves. We all had a
particular dive at which we excelled Mine was the back jack-knife.
For some reason it seemed easy and was almost perfectly executed
each time. One of the guys worked on a double flip after bouncing
on the board several times to gain enough height. We all tried every
dive but some of us never mastered more than three or four. Then the
inevitable happened. The plank snapped! Do you know how hard it
was to get a new plank? Not an easy overnight task. It usually took a
week or more to scout out the perfect one, then the usual clandestine
meetings and the casual moving of the plank a few steps each time it
was passed in order to move it to a more easily accessible location. This
was done in a nonchalant manner by casually using our feet to slide or
push the plank without bending over.

The lumber yard was situated between the harbor dockage and the
railroad yard because earlier loads of lumber came by barge or boat
and were unloaded at the dock. In later, years it came by rail. In our
detour through the yard we'd make a couple of plans for securing
our much needed equipment. Plan 'A' was to carry the plank with
the aid of several of the stronger boys, but plan 'B' was to drop it
into the water and float it down past the breakwater then over to our
dock. Usually plan 'A' was the one used: to get to the breakwater then
around the cove and down the tracks to the dock. Sounds simple,
doesn't it? Add darkness, mud, high tide, or the large rocks of the
railroad bed and you have a feat which ended up with scraped shins,
scratches from overhanging branches or stubbed toes, a challenge
superbly carried out by young, determined students of the river. I do
not recall if plan 'B' was ever used. Most of the guys showed up for
the installation and testing of the new board. Only once do I recall
obtaining a new un-weathered board. It was knot free, two full inches
thick and sixteen feet in length and fourteen to sixteen inches wide.
Most of our planks were twelve inches by one and a half inches by
twelve or fourteen feet long. I wasn't part of the crew obtaining it, but
I was there for the installation. A couple of dives to test it caused us
to become deliriously happy. It was dusk and too dark by the time we
finished. We were looking forward to finishing the clamping down

and getting a real bounce with a full two inch diving board. The next day we looked forward to using the new board and I imagine many dreams were had that night as we triumphantly anticipated all sorts of possibilities. When we got there about ten the next morning the plank had mysteriously disappeared. Someone had dug it up and took it away. Someone had come by boat and 'stolen' the hope of future Olympian divers. Replacing that particular board was almost impossible. It was the best we'd ever had. Miraculously our rivals across the river suddenly acquired a new board. I never spoke with them about how they acquired their board, but I suspect they watched and planned very carefully, laughing and joking about it. Inspecting the plank we found that they had nailed it to their dock making it impossible for us to reciprocate. Also, the dockage there was six to eight feet high, but the land was about three feet above the water. Somehow they had made an opening about six by four feet through the dockage arrangement, and this is where they placed the plank. They nailed it to the timbers and to the supporting braces, and also used rocks to weigh the plank down.

# CHAPTER III

## ON THE RIVER

About that time our father decided we needed a boat and came home with plans and the forms for a fourteen foot flat-bottomed row boat with one set of oarlocks. It had twenty-two inch sides making it more like a dory depth-wise. We built it in the back yard with our father's help when he had free time over the period of a few weeks. One of the jobs my brother and I had was to 'buck' the rivets along the strake while our father peened them. I think they were every two inches apart. The bow stem was double thick oak also riveted and screwed. The transom was also oak and reinforced for sturdiness. There were three thwarts or seats plus the rear seat. The ribs were oak and riveted. The gunwale was lined with a two inch wide oak strip that could be used as a handle when climbing into the boat from the water. It was a real beauty of a boat and was the envy of everyone on the river. It was launched and christened the 'Hadie Lou' about the time school let out for the summer. Needless to say, we learned to row and became quite adept in boatmanship. I suppose one of the reasons Pop made the boat was because several other kids had scows that were constantly bailed. But our boat never leaked after the initial swamping and swelling of the planking. It served as the flagship of the Viking force on the Thames for many years until we replaced it with a sixteen footer identically built. We had learned to row in the old scows, so this 'ship' allowed us to perfect our technique in small boat handling including sailing and navigating. Of course, the sail in most cases was a sheet or old blanket tied to the extra set of oars which were held up by two 'swabs' who would not have to row. We learned that there was such a condition as too much sail if the wind was very strong. It would pull the blanket sail out of your hands or lift you out of your seat, so shortening of the sail became a term we understood.

At first we went all over with our father as the steersman, or helmsman. He would sit in the stern and beat time while using an oar as the rudder. We eventually got good enough so that we were able pass a five horse-powered outboard motor with the "Hadie Lou II" with its two sets of oars. We lost because we didn't have the stamina to maintain the rugged pace needed to exceed a mile's distance. We were determined and occasionally in later years were to beat these guys over a mile or two because we'd switch rowers if we had a full crew. Sometimes we'd have four people rowing, two in the stern and two at the bow. The hard job was to figure out how to make the switch without going overboard. Timing and planning are everything. Usually, it was a casual row to the coves and islands that had been visited by Captain Kidd, Captain Blood, or some other swashbuckling privateer.

It was an exciting time, watching the maneuvers of the tugs and repositioning of dredgers and the connecting of pipes carrying the sand, mud and treasures galore. A favorite pastime was standing near the discharge pipe to see what popped out besides coal and sand. Occasionally a crab or eel would make it through unscathed, sometimes old shoes and a variety of sundry items too numerous to mention plus sand, sand, and more sand.

From this position to the left jog has been filled;
approximately eleven hundred feet

They filled in behind the breakwater, and our beloved mud-flats disappeared, as did the crabbing area, the minnow hatchery and eel pots. This put a damper on our crabbing and fishing during that summer and fall. It must have been in the late 30's or early 40's if I remember correctly. My brother and I estimated that it took almost ten years before there was a recovery to the pre-hurricane level of crabbing etc. One of the activities in which we indulged was to play and run on the floating sections of the dredge platforms containing the twelve inch pipes affixed to floats. They were large cylindrical steel tanks that looked like a hot water storage tank only longer about two feet in diameter severed as flotation devices. There was a wooden walk-way or cat-walk on top of the dredge-pipes that may have been thirty to fifty feet long. To us they seemed longer. There was also a railing on many but not all of the sections. The extra sections were stored and rafted in the cove until needed and were moved periodically to new locations. Sometimes they'd remain rafted in readiness for a week and our tag game took on new dimensions with new rules and more involvement, it was the advent of the alluring playground. Jumping from one cylinder to the other which was the only way to get from one section to another was hazardous to say the least. It always made us think of our abilities and prowess in leaping, especially if your sneakers were wet, which they usually were. The metal cylinders on which these contraptions sat were, as mentioned, roundish and the wet sneakers didn't adhere well to the painted wet steel. The end result was often a splash and you were automatically IT because you left the specific area of play. Oh yes, our rules were very specific about tagging on the three to five rafted platforms in the cove. There was no excuse for not navigating the hurdles correctly. Your error, you were IT.

The remains of our beloved cove after dredging and filling with sand, c. 2005

With the filled in area of sand came the notion of building a fort. We accomplished this by digging down five or six feet, obtaining railroad ties and carrying them a couple hundred feet. Then lining the walls so they would not collapse and putting other ties over the top for a roof with only a space left as an entrance. We covered the roof with sand. To prevent the sand from filtering through, I think we used cardboard. This may not seem like the best way, but remember this was done by ten, eleven, and twelve year olds! I recall that the ties were heavy and a lot of planning had to be done to accomplish this feat.

That night with candles, matches, Bugler (the five cent package), and a cigarette roller from someone's father, we went to our hideout fort. The hatch was opened and the first one put his hands on each side of the hatch and lowered himself down without uttering a sound.

I have also forgotten how many boys were there, but the most amazing thing was that not one person had uttered a sound until the last one had dropped into waist deep water! We had dug it at the start of an ebbing tide, finished it at low tide, so when we went back at the flood tide it was filled with water. What a disappointment. And the bugler got wet! "YOU DID WHAT?! You could have been drowned!"

One incident made the newspaper, which was read to us the next morning. The newspaper article stated that the fire department has had many strange calls but one of the strangest calls was when they responded to a huge fire on the sand south of the lumber and freight yards. The location is almost a mile from the bridge along the tracks to the point in question. Every bit of scrap wood, crates, tires, some railroad ties and trees, were piled at least ten feet high, and the collection had taken several days. About ten of us were sitting around when the trucks came bouncing, and I mean bouncing along the tracks with lights and sirens. The breeze was out of the south, so we didn't hear them till they were almost upon us. We had no idea that we were the cause of all the commotion. The paper continued that it turned out to be a colored man, Auster Banderson, and his children having a crab roast or fish roast. Auster Banderson and two others were colored, the rest of us were white. "You Did What? You were there?" That wasn't so bad because we reminded them that we had mentioned a 'bonfire', but this was more than a bonfire—Guess sometimes you can't win.

Once when we were walking down the tracks they were unloading water melons. These had been packed in straw and through the ride a few had been cracked and were unusable, so the crew unloading them gave some to us because we had helped them. We ate some there and took the rest home. On another occasion we helped them unload a whole car load of melons so this time they said, "You boys worked hard," so they gave each of us an unbroken melon. PK took his home and his father looked at it, rotated it in his hands and said. in a definite Polish accent, "You steal! No 'kuuracks'! You steal mel-lones!" No Papa, No. and the rest of the kids said the same but to no avail. PK was chained to the third floor porch with the statement that, 'You no steal no more!' His father thought he had broken into the boxcar, so he literally chained PK to the porch for a week. It was supposed to have been longer. We'd stand down below and talk to him until we were chased away by his father. A bucket of water coming over the railing unannounced spoke very loudly. Lessons were learned by all. The innocent are sometimes punished for the guilty. Or is that by the guilty? In any event, we told our parents about it but they never said, 'HE DID WHAT?' Unfortunately we hadn't told our parents about PK for close to a week, but I noticed that shortly after talking to them, PK was released, or rather unchained. Did they say something? My father was a very compassionate man and disliked seeing injustices metered out to the innocent. Once when he was walking on the West Side, he witnessed a police officer being attacked by three men. My father waded in to help the policeman. The paddy wagon came and put my father in with the three criminals. It wasn't until he got to the police station that the victim officer said, "NO, not him, he helped me!" Back to the River the indisputable ruler of our lives, especially during the late spring to early fall.

The 'Hadie Lou II' without question gave us unequivocal dominance with its extra length and capacity. Everyone wanted to ride, row or go on excursions to those remote and isolated areas of intrigue: marshes, islands, coves and bridges. How many people have ever seen the underside of the bridges reasonably close? We saw a great variety of boats underway; innumerable barges in tow, tankers and coal in transit and a variety of mud-flats and sand bars at different tides. We saw the deflection of water off obstacles, the beauty of sunrises and sunsets at each of these places. During storms, whether light or heavy rain and with or without wind, the river kept calling to us. The list could go on, but we let the River be our guide on innumerable days. I have to give my parents credit for allowing us the freedom to make wise choices about the River. Of course, there were times when we didn't get our chores done and that would end with a punishment involving the River and Her calling. A terrible punishment was to be banned from riverside activities.

# CHAPTER IV

## UP THE RIVER

Today I went on an excursion, it was delightful. At 0843 hours we entered the channel after leaving the Merry Hall docking facility and headed south to Fisher's Island Sound. It had been years since I sailed this course on the Pawcatuck River. Our destination was the Thames River, from its mouth to its source, at the merging of three streams; the Shetucket, the Yantic, and the Falls which was a continuation of the Yantic around Hollyhock Island. This forms the Norwich Harbor and the beginning of the Thames. We arrived at our destination around eleven hundred hours, and tied up to the dockage there to eat lunch after having meandering up the Shetucket to within a few hundred feet of the East Side bridge. Following a leisurely meal, we proceeded up to the falls mill, idling along at a flood tide and a perigee tide at that. Good thing, most of it is clear and navigable, compared to what it was 5 years ago, when it had branches, crates and old tires in the way. The old auto bridge has been replaced, but the old bridge abutments are till there, as well as the old railroad bridge foundations. Further up, ust before the mill, the old water pipe crosses over to the west side. is rusted, but there had been a new section replacement to part it. Most of the shore to the east is nicely kept, but the Hollyhock and side still looks dilapidated and is in need of a clean-up. The old eam or channel that had cut through there is gone hidden filled or camouflaged. The Episcopal Church (see page 67) still looks grand and stately. It was built on the site of an old cemetery which they tell me was dug up and moved elsewhere. Back to the past . . . to the memories jogged while making the turn at the New London Light.

The light area remains the same, but from there up river, the shoreline has been altered considerably. No, not caused by the River, for its course, believe it or not, is pretty much the same. None of the Breakwaters were in evidence, but they may well have been under water due to the perigee tide, or maybe they pulled them all up for some reason or other. A mystery for the moment! Any changes that occurred south of Allyn's Point would not be noticeable to me, but north of that location, there is an alteration that I never would have believed. It seems that a few of the islands are gone or reduced in size; the ones at The Draw-Bridge are still very much in the same relative position they were 65 years ago. The Draw-Bridge itself has been rebuilt and doesn't quite look the same, and the banks of the River are over grown with shrubs and trees. Some of the islands are now connected to the land and overgrown. Even the island that had the old apple tree is now part of the peninsula! The old water tower that furnished the water for the steam engine is long gone, and there is no evidence of even the site foundations or the milk-house. Perhaps a closer examination may reveal their exact location, which means we would have to walk the tracks. There may be an access road from the hospital area that would save a great deal of time. There was a road there once; it was used to deliver milk to the old milk-house near the water tank. Another reason the train stopped; milk pickup.

Anyway, when I get the photos back, I'll peruse them and make notations accordingly, but for the time being, we'll mention the obvious. After the Draw-Bridge there was no evidence of the breakwaters. Some of the channel makers were there, howbeit rebuilt, but their locations were in the same relative positions, but NO BREAKWATERS! Whatever happened to them all? The next most important location was Trading Cove. That bridge is still relatively the same, although it looks revitalized. Perhaps new timbers have been installed, but it is still wooden as I remembered it. The beach on the cove-side was completely under water. I have very fond memories of that beach and the trail that led down to it. The trail had long been abandoned, there were no signs of its existence. Perhaps closer inspection may enlighten us. After passing Trading-Cove, we rounded the bend and the small islands along the west side came into view. The next cove-let was where there had been a river-side shack beyond the breakwater. Gone, but what had been the old light-house and marker were still there. It was in relatively the same place, albeit reconstructed on a pile of large rocks, but again no barriers breakwaters. From Trading Cove we were able to see up to the old Thermos Co. and the Woolen Mill. The desolation is all I could think of when we viewed the Woolen Mill area. Even the buildings were torn down. The third story windows in the mill were smashed. It looked as though rocks had been thrown through them, but even the best arm could not have reached that far. Perhaps someone broke in and smashed them from the inside.

Thermos company from the old Coal Wharf

The wooden docks were in great disrepair and almost unrecognizable from their previous state of grandeur. The Thermos dock is in a similar state; gone for all practical purposes. Again, the loving breakwater was nowhere to be seen, if it exist at all. I still suspect that they are all there but not visible because of the perigee tide.

(Returning a few days later confirmed the existence of breakwaters in all their glory, although the tops were no longer flat but rather irregular, indicating the movement of the stones due to weather and wave action. I suspect that freezing and thawing probably moved the flat stones to their current locations.

# CHAPTER V

## LANDMARKS ALONG THE RIVER

Another adventure that came along with the advent of the boat was to occasionally go pick up our Pop at the G&E (Gas and Electric) plant where he was employed. There was a small dock or landing area at the lower portion of the plant just before the electric department and we'd maneuver through the rocks, especially at lower tides. We tried to remember where the rocks were for high tide, and slack water. There was quite a current during ebb tide and rapids were definitely there, but so was the remnant of a channel, which we finally found. We later tried at low tide a few times, but the current was really too swift and it involved using the oars as poles to reach the pick-up point. We passed under a railroad bridge on the way, and wondered how the city would look if we climbed up to the top. The steel was about a foot wide and easy to climb up and over. The bridge was about 40 feet high; what a view! We could see Dottie's house very clearly from there. There were times when we'd get into shallow water only eight inches deep, not a good situation, but the positive side is that we could hop out and push or use the rope to pull the boat the 50 feet needed to get into the pick-up zone. Eventually it was a pick up during the flood tides, until we got a motor. Some of the early pickups at various locations were quite memorable. Jumping off the boat with a line to tie up onto the 12"x12" timbers that lined the banks the first time, was unforgettable. Most of the other timbers were only 8"x8". These tar soaked timbers extruded creosote in small sticky pools and when you hopped onto them with bare feet, you'd have instant black tattoos. It's almost un-removable, probably a reason we could run barefooted down the tracks was because we had a coating of dirt and tar on our soles almost permanently. We could easily identify with the old story between the black footed and white footed Indian tribes. These distinguishing features were between those who lived along the tracks and docks versus those from the wooded hills area. A similar problem developed when the roads were resurfaced or tarred. Somebody from our group got the idea to chew tar that was without grains of sand in it, so we tried that also. I don't know where the idea was conceived, probably from picking up a glob of gum that was discarded, and picked up to chew, only to find a grain of sand in it. You never retrieved a glob of gum off the street to chew? Gosh sometimes it was hardly devoid of flavor. Wintergreen was the most desired flavor. That's why you sniffed it first. We discovered wintergreen through our mother's knowledge of plants; she pointed out these berries on one of our Sunday forays. Anyway, we chewed tar on occasion, especially the type on the old roads that looked clear of sand grains. The stuff on the ties and dockage had an odor different from the road tar and was not a good taste. Most likely it was the creosote. All this because of landing on hot tar extruded from dock timbers. The first thing you thought of when stepping into it was to jump into the water! That sort of helped it congeal and solidify the glob and reduce the pain. Sometimes it peeled off, but usually it just had to wear off. Of course in time we learned that gasoline did dissolve the tar to some extent. That was one of the advantages of wearing KEDS. There were one or two other advantages; when walking the rails, the high sided KEDS protected your ankles if you slipped off the rail. Another was when walking in the woods, you were protected from thorns. Toward the end of the summer when the tread was worn down, a thorn had been known to penetrate the sole. Was that the second year use of the KEDS? (It all depended on how much you grew during the winter.).

Naturally most of the kids tripped periodically, because their parents would buy a shoe at least one size larger, if not two, so you could 'grow into' them. The same prevailed for winter shoes, especially 'high cuts' that were donated! I tried to get two years out of my favorite pair. They resembled what the lumber-jacks and the Royal Canadian Mounted Police wore. My feet were so cramped I could hardly walk, but to me they were indicative of an adventurer, the emulation of heroes. Someone had given me a hand me down pair of riding breeches, so with that combination I was the cat's meow. In reality, I was a rag-a-muffin, an urchin with spirit. The 'high-cuts' had been recently 'tapped', so you had to get your money's worth out of them. I guess one of my brothers became the eventual recipient of them.

Speaking of tapping, have you ever had a sole lose the stitching and the whole sole to the heel would be free? And by taking a step, you could flick your foot in such a way to snap the sole so it came up and slapped the bottom of the shoe before you stepped on it. It also was a way of getting rid of sand or pebbles caught in between the shoe and its sole. Some kids went for weeks like that and could be distinguished by their characteristic flapping when they walked. This taught you to avoid puddles, snow and slush. What duct-tape would have meant at that time. Stitching or using the old holes for the stitching was a common activity when you wanted to repair your shoes. Waxed thread and sometimes wire was used to refasten the sole to the edges. Newspaper, also cardboard was not unheard of being stuffed into the shoe to keep you warm or reasonably dry while going to school, especially if you had cut the flap off. Many homes had lasts which are metal foot-shaped items for putting the shoe on for tapping and shoe repair was a common activity. Special boxes of nails were a common commodity in many homes. That was a good thing about the summer and living along the river . . . no shoes, but new Keds, which we didn't wear too often in the boat unless there were crabs crawling around.

Upstream sewer above swimming and dock area

An adventure that is unparalleled was one that required a low tide, also known as an ebbing tide. There was a tunnel, rectangular in shape, the height was approximately twice the width, or close to that—about a 2x4 opening, and lined on all four sides, a floor and two sides. The overhead or 'ceiling' with variously sized cut or quarried stones rectangular in shape and fitted. The question was how far into its depths could we go to discover the end or source of the very shallow stream that exited the tunnel. Visibility was restricted after 10 to 15 feet, so some sort of light would be needed for this exploration. Algae or moss grew on the floor, making it quite slippery for a little way up, and one had to grasp the rock sides for support. The furthest I ever got was about twenty five feet. The flashlights were not much use because the sunlight reflected inside and caused blindness which rendered our flashlights, with very weak batteries, practically useless.

Swim area filled with sediment, brook and downstream sewer opening

Brook and sewer opening

I do not recall the furthest distance anyone attained and finally decided that the sewers of Paris were different from ours. This outlet was for the houses in our immediate locale. We tried to discover how long it would take for various household ingredients to reach the outlet. To accomplish this we wrote notes or put a distinguishing article into the toilet, flushed it and then ran down the hill to join the crew waiting there at the riverside opening to see when it would arrive, or whose notes would arrive first! This consumed quite a bit of time, and some of the guys claimed they could distinguish from the sounds whose toilet flushed. This is doubtful because all I could ever hear was rushing water. Of course, this could only be accomplished at low tide for at high tide the opening was almost completely filled with water. We all seemed to have a high tolerance to disease. Our immune systems seemed to function superbly due to exposures to a variety of organisms. We never fully understood why the other guys never came to swim at our location. Eventually we did understand and wondered how we were able to live through it all. LUCKY!

Another good thing about the River, we almost always knew what time it was as long as the wind was from the right direction or there was no wind at all. I don't know if I had ever seen a wristwatch, and a pocket watch was too expensive to own. I marveled at parents who would say be home by three o'clock and no one had a watch. Clocks were not displayed anywhere except in some stores, but we had the tide and each mill had a whistle that would sound at the same time each day. We knew the different sounds produced by the various mills. Some had sirens. Another way we told time was from the passing trains. They followed a definite schedule, and adhered to it religiously. If I recall, the three o'clock freight was always on time. It stopped for water at the water tower near the State Hospital, and would be on its way within fifteen minutes. Later there was a four o'clock train that travelled north and slowed for the tunnel and railroad bridge in the center of town. Another train, the 'Silver Steak', was a passenger train that came south bound around two PM. Another that I remember was at eleven in the evening. Usually we were asleep for that one, but on occasion we witnessed its passing, and tried to count the cars. That was another pastime, counting railroad cars. There were other trains that ran pretty much on schedule, but these peaked my interest. Across the river there was the C.V. (Central Vermont) that had a similar schedule but they seemed to be trains of a shorter length. There were quite a few accidents involving trains and cars at the crossings in the woolen mill area, and a few years later I was a witness to one when we moved to the other side of the "River"; not a pretty sight.

Gangs abounded throughout the town, and many stories existed about their prowess, uncanny abilities, and toughness. One story that brought knowledge of their existence and brought them notoriety was the creation of playgrounds, and their installations in various parts of towns. These stimulated organizations of baseball and volleyball teams, plus horseshoes which created a competitive rivalry. We also joined the playground functions, mostly because of the playground teacher. Her first name was Mary, and her last name began with an 'L'. She was only a few years older than some of us, and many of the guys had a crush on her. She could have told us to do almost anything and it would have been a successful endeavor. I wasn't as smitten with her as were some of the others. The river was more my 'mistress' and more alluring, but belonging to the playground did open my eyes to the existence of groups other than the 'Bums' and us, the 'River Rats'. There were two or three gangs who had notorious stories that preceded them and instilled a sort of fear or a hardy respect, or maybe even an admiration of them. Traveling into their domain for baseball always energized us and stimulated our alertness. We had heard stories about New York Dead End Kids and identified the new 'city groups' with that image, thereby magnifying their deeds and instilling fear of them. Were the truth to be known, they were no different from us and the stories were blown out of proportion. Years later while talking with one of the most fearful group members from a certain street area, he mentioned that there was only one group they feared. It was the 'River Rats'. US! Unbelievable. Hence, the wild stories were just that, 'wild stories' that were eventually put to rest, though there were friendly discussions and confessions. We knew that was the truth when we got to high school and played on the same teams.

When the 'Hadie Lou' (our boat) was launched, we began our exploration of the river in detail. That must have been in the late 30's, (1937-1938). It was a summer to remember. Our excursions were of quite a variety. Pop had rowed to Allyn's Point for a camping trip which was a new adventure! We spent the first night on a point opposite the drawbridge, then on to Allyn's Point the next day after a home cooked meal over our campfire. We had no formal camping gear, maybe a couple of blankets, and if I recall correctly, it was a chilly night in May. Pop worked a rotating shift and had various weekends free, and this must have been one of those weekends. I recall wearing short pants and being cold. The next day we made for Allyn's Point. It was warm by then and we arrived by noon to set up camp near a cabin that was there but it sure wasn't much of a cabin. Pop had secured permission to use it from the owner, a reason for this destination. We had left on Friday afternoon after Pop had finished work. Most of the gear was stowed in the boat before he arrived home so with great anticipation we awaited his arrival. Many of the details about the trip are long forgotten, but the trip back was the most memorable. Early in the morning of our departure for the return trip, the wind was out of the north, and the tide was about to ebb. We started to row, but the headwind was too great, so Pop took over and gave it his best. We made the docking facility near the hospital, and by that time the tide was also against us, hence we made very little headway, just about nil. Pop was exhausted and the wind was more out of the NNW, pushing us against the wharf and pilings as well as the combination of the outgoing tide. It was a disaster. We tried using a rope to pull the boat while two of us held the boat off the piling, but nothing seemed to work. We tried all sorts of combinations and finally in the slight lee of a group of pilings adjacent to the dock area we tied the boat up and left it to be picked up another day. We walked home along the tracks carrying what we could manage feeling a little dejected that we had to leave Hadie Lou.

A rock island looking south toward Norwich State Hospital

We returned the next day and retrieved the boat that had some scraping (chafing) on it due to it rubbing on the pilings. That taught us a valuable lesson and we utilized that knowledge when we encountered shallow water and needed to pull the boat along the shore with a rope; someone needed to hold the boat off the shore with an oar while standing in her. I suspect that the reason we were not successful at the docking area was that the dock was at least six to eight feet above the water at that time and that the angle of tow was too great. (Not enough scpoe) If we had been level with the boat and the dock as we were when we were on shore, it might well have been successful.

One of the lesser known facts about the River was the existence of 'breakwaters' which apparently are called 'dikes' on today's charts. Some of them were close to a mile or more along the river, one being opposite the Trading Cove. The River channel was lined with breakwaters that had sections that would form a network of deflectors that controlled the altering of the channel and limited the depositing of silt and sand, allowing the build-up of mud flats and sand bars within the breakwater barriers. There were openings twenty to thirty feet from either the channel breakwater or the shore. One had to snake back and forth, a distance of perhaps one hundred to two hundred feet, through the grid-work of perpendicular but strategically placed barriers. these were approximately three to four hundred feet or more apart. There were mini-channels that did not allow you to cut diagonally across or you got stuck-in-the-mud. Several of the openings on the land side were so shallow that one could not get the boat through at low tide. There were rocks strategically placed so water would run, but no craft could get through, not even a kayak. These we lifted over if necessary. Within these areas there was eelgrass and other algae types growing, and we'd go there to trap minnows, scoop crabs, or travel within the confines of the protection of the barriers from headwinds on rough days when the channel was too rough. We'd tow the boat with a rope as we walked along the breakwater until we got to a place where the top rocks had shifted or where some tug or barge had dislodged them and that meant getting wet or getting back into the boat and bypassing the ten to twenty feet of unsafe travel. Taking the mud flat-sandbar route was like traveling a maze. The most important thing was to remember where the small channels were, then travel down river to the openings that could be used. Those openings would take you to your destination. There should be an award given to the memory of those early engineers for their foresight and their planning

Breakwaters are extremely important. One illustration refers to the St. John's River in Florida, from DeLand to Jacksonville. When shipping took place years ago, they would often run aground at various locations. They would have to unload the boat completely, then they would sail on while the freight was transferred across the isthmus to the other side. While the boat, now lightened, safely made its way around the meander and shallows, they would have to reload and continue. It would take up to six weeks to make the trip. With the advent of dredging and pilings and breakwaters, the time was reduced to fourteen hours Now we can look forward to fresh oranges!

One of our many trips was to go down the River to an opening, then go toward shore to explore. What looked to be a great little island turned out to be a ledge with shrubs growing out of the cracks. There went our dreams of digging for buried treasure, and discovering Captain Kidd, or Blood's booty! Another destination was behind a small island at a peninsula, hiding a great apple tree, the boughs of which hung over the water. At the proper tide one could put in there to get green apples. The bow would actually be on the shore but also under the spreading boughs. From the river side you could not be seen, so no one else on the river would suspect its existence. We also knew that on a really windy day, if we could manage to get to this area, we could literally drag the boat home through the network of breakwaters. There were times when we'd forget the lowering tide and get trapped because the water was too low, but that barrier was only about a quarter of a mile from the mooring area. Leaving the boat there was no problem. We just had to remember to get it at the proper tide, or just wait there for the tide to change. On occasion we'd try to cross these flats by sliding the boat over the mud flats but that was a disaster. We'd be up over our knees in mud and have no leverage, we just kept slipping and falling in black mire and that was not always pleasant. Sometimes it was humorous and occasionally initiated a mud fight. We also learned to walk across mud flats without sinking into the mud. Ever try that? Simple. Just go on your knees! The lower leg and foot with your toes extended acts like a snow-shoe, balancing your weight toward the middle of your legs, so you could slide along to reach your desired location. Once we learned this, getting to and from the breakwater in the cove from the shore was no problem. If you didn't mind getting a little wet. Actually, you'd only get wet from the knees down but with shorts, who cared. We found it was better to have long pants on to avoid scratches or cuts from shells, sticks, or glass.

Along the river all the breakwaters had lighthouse structures at important junctures. They had cement foundations on top of carefully stacked and cut granite rocks. These were similar to the ones that were stacked to make the breakwaters. Their colors were red and white or black and white. The one on our side at the point was red, and between them were the cans or nuns. Today the coloring is different, and recently after a brief trip, I saw they seem to still be in the relatively same position they were years ago.

Before the advent of a motor, we were quite familiar with the river which was between one and one half miles north to three or four miles south. Most of the breakwater barriers were on our side of the river from our dock area to the drawbridge. The exception is the hospital area where the oil tankers would unload. A frequent destination of ours was the trading cove for the water there was clearer making both fishing and crabbing good. We could make it down in less than an hour and back in an hour plus, unless the tide was right. We tried to plan with that in mind. Sometimes we would dive off the trestle and swim there. We thought we were Johnny Weissmuller all over again. The whole family would go and meet at the Trading Cove area. We went by boat since we didn't have a car while the other family members would drive or take the trolley or bus to the area and walk down the dirt road to the beach for an outing. The Fourth of July was celebrated this way for several years, the first being in 1938. I recall my cousins being there and other family members. Actually, I think this was the year I had a black eye from falling on some stairs while carrying a watermelon. I probably had tripped because my shoes were too big and rather than let go of the melon, I bent my head and in doing so hit it on the tread cutting my eyebrow. When I think back it was the same eyebrow that my brother had broken a milk bottle on many years earlier. I learned not to antagonize my brother at an early age. I still don't know what precipitated the initial assault but, 'c'est la vie'. Over the years, trading cove played an important part in our lives.

One activity that we indulged in was to hitch a ride back from the drawbridge or trading cove by rowing real fast to get behind a barge and let it drag us along! The water coming up from under the stern of the barge would sort of roll up and toward the stern thereby pulling us along. a vacuum-like action. We would sit in the stern of our boat with an oar as a rudder to keep the bow-stem up almost if not touching the barge stern to keep us in line without being dragged broadside to the stern. We'd ride that way all the way up river to our mooring area, then push off with an oar to get out of the draft. I'm sure that the attendants allowed us to ride that way many times.

# CHAPTER VI

## HURRICANE OF 1938

## AND THE RAILROAD TRACKS

We didn't really have a dock area, because the best two or three places were taken by other squatters. For our mooring, we had just flat stones with a gravel spot about three or four feet in width. and there may have been a metal rebar protruding from a rock drill hole that we used for tying the bow. The stern was attached to the anchor rope which was tossed out and made fast. Eventually we put in a mooring which we tied to the stern, with a quick release of the proper length for both bow and stern.

September finally came and that meant the boat had to come out of the water for winter storage. School had started and it ruled. The boat was reluctantly hauled and moved across the three or four sets of rails, then up a short roadway and left to be placed on a dolly for transport to the winter storage area. The area in which we left the boat was about fifteen feet above the River at high tide. That weekend we were due to move the Hadie Lou to her winter haven. It was safe for the moment, but that didn't last long. My brother had a job and was working as a delivery boy for a grocer. During those days one could call in an order to a grocer, or send a note and they would deliver your groceries. Usually they were delivered in a cardboard box, or a bushel basket and carried by a delivery-boy.

School was let out early this day because a northeaster was brewing, and was reaching its height. I credit Miss Kilroy with the school closing. She was frightened because of the trees being blown down, in the adjacent yard It was so intense that the grocer had someone drive his car while my brother hopped out to deliver the groceries and collect the money. There was a wooden fence encircling the school yard, made of vertical slats. This was destroyed and my brother and a few others cleaned it up, carrying it home for firewood.

The oak tree endangering the house in '38

Suddenly, trees started to fall. We were concerned about a huge tree just above our house on the high side as you came out the front door. I was home with my mother and when we looked out from our home to the river my mother said we should go check the boat in case the water came that high. It looked as if it were already over the tracks. A couple of days prior we had pulled our boat from the river getting it ready to carry it to the house for winter storage. That poor old flat bottom fourteen foot row boat with two sets of oars, and one set of oarlocks was still the queen of the river; the Hadie Lou. The boat had been left upside down just over the tracks where there were two set of rails plus the spurs, and near the dirt road that swung around there. Crown Hill is now paved.

We went down and sure enough, the water was over the tracks and then some. The boat was floating upside down and almost seventy-five feet out. White caps were evident where the channel would normally have been. Oil cases were floating down as well as stacks of lumber from the lumber yard. A rope was tied around my waist and I swam out through floating debris, sticks, branches and leaves, where I tied the rope to the bow ring, swam to the stern and started kicking for all I was worth to push the 'Hadie Lou' shoreward.

Good thing I left my 'Keds' and long pants on, because of all the sticks and leaves I was kicking. My mother was up over her knees in water hauling on the rope to drag us to shore. Remember at that time women didn't wear slacks or pants so you can imagine her standing with her dress in the water and hauling away. She had pulled her dress from behind, between her legs, tucked it into her belt like a diaper and stood with her rolled stocking just above her knees.

We tied the boat to a tree and left it; a few minutes more and the 'Hadie Lou' would have been in the current being carried down-stream and gone The white caps looked to be about five to seven or eight feet high. There in the middle of it all was a stack of two by fours being swept down-stream with a man on top trying to get to the other shore by poling or paddling with a two by four. The stack looked to be over fifteen feet high. He eventually did make it but what happened to the stack of two by fours is something I never found out.

It was a strange episode in our relationship with the river. The wind was out of the south one minute, then out of the north the next. Branches were flying and trees were bending almost in half with their tops touching the ground. Walking was a problem. We backed into the wind when it changed direction.

My father didn't come home that night. He worked at the gas company and unbeknownst to us, he had saved the gas company plant by shutting down the generator. Otherwise, there would have been an explosion that could have a chain reaction throughout the town. He had crawled over the deep swirling water on a super heated six to eight inch steam pipe with rags on his hands and knees so he wouldn't get burned. People had gas in their homes, but no electricity.

He never mentioned what he had done; we learned of it second hand one day years later. On one of my visits, he explained and showed me what he had done when I asked about it. There were several unsung heroes at the plant that day, but Pop was the most important in my eyes but then, I'm prejudiced.

My brother arrived shortly after we reached home and told us that a tree had fallen on the car between the front and back seats. We went to look at the car the next day, climbing over and under trees to get to the crushed car. It was a miracle that no one was injured.

We walked the tracks the following day, picking up whatever we could find that we thought was valuable. Oil cans that had been washed downstream from the oil storage area were littering the shores and the area on the hillside of the tracks. We picked up what we could and a man came along and offered us money if we carried them up to his house which we did. We made fifty cents. We thought he was going to return the cans, but later discovered he never did!

His home was three hundred feet up a sixty degree hill overlooking the river. Not a very nice guy. His home was also burglarized a few years later and he lost a very valuable coin collection. The culprits were caught and we knew all of them. It was a sort of a "dare you" stunt. All the boys were county home residents and all from one family. The two younger boys were conned into the activity by an older brother so they were really the innocent victims. However, they paid the price by going to reform school in Cheshire. I always wondered what happened to the one who was my age. I wonder if the man who was robbed should have been prosecuted.

After the storm, there was no transportation for a week. The tracks and the roads were only open in certain areas, plus there were patrols at night to prevent looting. I doubt any one had that in mind, but the patrols were more for the safety of the locals. Even the Boy Scouts were called out. They ran messages and were even stationed at dangerous intersections. We had no lights for about a week but we had kerosene lamps and we did have gas so cooking was not a problem because we had a wood/coal stove in the kitchen. It was a gas range also, so we were in good shape, and it wasn't cold enough to require the furnace for heat.

The date was September 21, 1938. The famous hurricane of 1938! Yes, I swam in a hurricane and my brother delivered groceries. Clean up was a many person effort and everyone pitched in without thought of getting paid. Families got together and helped each other. No one missed school much except perhaps the super students. The shortest route to the city school was along the railroad tracks. The main road had several hills and some curves, so it was easier and faster trip to go along our beloved river.

Our neighborhood school only had six grades, so we had to eventually go to the inner-city school for seventh and eighth grades. It was a little over a mile in distance. The high school was another half mile past that. We walked both ways, and didn't carry a lunch during the grade school days. No wonder we were in better shape than most kids today. But by going to the city school we felt as though we were invading the neighborhood in the middle of town. Each time I crossed the bridge into town I felt as though I was in another country. One of my last looks each day was to the river and the tracks as I disappeared between the concrete and brick walls of the buildings.

Occasionally we'd walk the tracks through the tunnel and over the railroad bridge to the station and the square. Then we continued to school past the courthouse but that route was frowned on by officials and our parents. We used the same route when we went to high school and one of the highlights taking that route was that they would unload the new cars that were shipped from the Detroit plants and we'd see the newest autos before anyone else.

Tunnel view toward switch yard from railroad bridge

Franklin Square at turn of century

Exiting the tunnel to a bridge with a great view

Yes, cars had headlights in the fenders. It was not a rumor. In 1939, an uneasiness developed in the fall of that year. Hitler made headlines and there was a division of loyalties among families in our town. Most of the kids had no allegiance but their parents did and they eventually pitted themselves against the German and Italian families even though they'd been citizens for a hundred or more years. This was especially true for the Polish and French Canadian and Jews toward any descendants of the Germans' and Italians. What painful unjustified name calling and fist fights ensued, and no one can possible understand the injustices that prevailed during that period. Finally it was decided that those people were Americans and had no connection with the Nazis' or Fascists' persuasion. That may have been the year that we could finally afford an outboard motor for our boat before the advent of gas and food rationing. With the gas rationing there was the return to the propulsion method of earlier days, but that wasn't until the '40's.

The switchyard or what remains of it

The railroad switch yard was only about a half mile from our home, so we knew what was shipped by rail and what was not. Again at the end of the year, we saw the newest model cars before anyone else in town other than the men unloading and the dealers. To unload a boxcar from the middle door was a tricky maneuver and we heard some colorful language from the workers which we repeated to our parents. Bad mistake on our part!

We'd been warned about the dangers of hopping freights. We watched carefully how they coupled and uncoupled box cars and flat cars, tank cars and coal cars, and how they released the air so the brakes would function correctly. We saw how they set the torpedoes and why they put them one, two, or three in a row, and how far apart they put them. We were told not to ever touch one of them. We watched them put in new ties when they tamped the road bed, and being curious we asked what they would do with the old ties they had stacked. Occasionally we'd 'borrow' one but a few years later we would use these ties to build a fort. Yes, you'd think we'd have learned our lesson the first time, but we were proud of our accomplishments. I don't think my father was as upset as my mother, and I think they only said it because they were expected to be alarmed.

Notice the height of the ladder

One of our friends slipped and were it not for his agility and quick thinking he would have lost an arm or even his life. It was a dangerous and foolish endeavor on all our parts but it should be mentioned and emphasized that it should not be attempted! We watched brakemen hop on freights and walk the length of trains while the trains were moving; we also watched them walk along the trains checking the brakes and couplings and hoses to see if the safety features were in order. We'd walk with them, and at times they were entertaining and informative about the switching, the changeovers and the torpedoes. Torpedoes were explosive devices that were put on the tracks and they exploded when an engine went over them, making a loud sound to warn the engineer. There may have been one, two or three depending upon the warning needed, and they were attached to the rail by lead strips 3"x ¼" that wrapped over the rail. We'd pick up the strips after the train passed and use them as sinkers when fishing. We learned about the lights, the assembly of cars in the yard, and of the switching engines. Most of the brakemen were quite knowledgeable about the doings of young men and their needs. They always warned us about the danger of the yard work, staying alert and listening.

One thing to listen for was the chain reaction of a starting train; you could hear the alteration of the couplings going from one position to another at the start. You see when it stopped, the hook of the coupling rested against the car in front. There was a space, so that the pulling away was a jerk by the engine. The one inch space clunked or clanked on the hook of the car behind and it gave a staccato clanking reaction along the fifty to one hundred car assembly. You could hear it from almost a quarter mile away. We all attempted to hop freights. A big No-No. This was especially after that boy had slipped. The big mistake was to try it from the high side. Actually he should never have tried it at all from any location. But, hindsight is always enlightening. He fell as his foot slipped on the step and he landed on the track with his right arm on the track and saw the wheel coming. He quickly rolled away from the tracks in a spinning motion that took him to the second set of tracks. As he got up the adrenalin was pumping so fast that he just rolled to his feet and at that exact moment someone, a brakeman who was not visible when the boy went to hop, grabbed him, but the boy spun out of his grasp and took off up the tracks into the shrubs and home. He said he never had such a frightening experience. Did he ever try it again? Yes, but with extreme caution, and slower moving trains.

As you can see, you don't hop from this side!

Most of us tried hopping and some became quite adept at it and eventually worked for the railroad. We would hop on the outside of a car, because if the caboose was close and we never knew how close that would be, they could see on the inside of a curve as the cars passed it, but they couldn't see on the outside, so we'd hop accordingly. Then we would slip around the end of the car to the inside ladder and remain there until we were ready to hop off, or the train came to a stop. Usually we'd ride toward the water tank where the train would stop to take on water; it then proceeded southward. We'd wait for the four o'clock and ride it back to the yard or before the tunnel or bridge and hop off and go home or wherever our next adventure took us. On occasion we'd hop the wrong one and end up near Allyn's Point where the train slowed. Then, we would have to struggle back one way or another. Once in awhile the trains were lined up in the yard and if the switching engine wasn't there, we would climb the cars and have a game of tag on the catwalks. We could jump from one line of cars to the other, but only at special places. We were never destructive and never opened a car door if it had a seal on it, but we were adventurous. We were caught once or twice and verbally reprimanded with a friendly caution by the brakemen or trainmen. We looked up to them.

We'd heard about railroad detectives and always supposed someone walking the tracks might be one if we didn't recognize the walk. Yes, we learned to watch and to be able to identify one or more by their walk. Hobos were occasionally in our area and they had a sort of lean-to hide-away in a vine covered tree area in an alcove of the cliff on our end of the yard. When we thought no one was around we'd venture into it and look around. There were just old oil-cloth table coverings, cans and bottles. It merely served as a shelter from the elements for a day or so until they got a job or caught their next 'reserved' train.

Later when the river was dredged and the area was filled with sand in the cove, we'd have bonfires and cook or roast fish, eels, or crabs. Some of the hobos would come down to get warm and we'd share our food with them. A few were pretty grimy looking and perhaps we were also, so I supposed it evened out. We'd catch shiners or minnows and roast them on a fire after cleaning them and rinsing them in the water from which we caught them. No one had a knife to decapitate them, so we improvised. A stick went through the length of the fish and then was roasted. I have no idea how many semi-raw fish were consumed.

Discipline was regulated by whether you followed directions for accomplishing your tasks, chores, deeds or rather NOT getting them done. Restrictions were usually the way discipline was administered, but occasionally spankings, or lickings were metered out. Spankings were to the butt while lickings were to the legs. Both involved a belt or a switch cut or broken off from a nearby bush. Pop had the fastest "whipping off of a belt" in the east. Until Pop gained weight and almost lost his pants. Then we had more warning and could depart if necessary. A few kids had parents that were abusive and not as lucky as we were. One could witness the bruises or marks at the swimming area. Saturday and Sunday mornings were the times when these would be seen, because Fridays and Saturdays were paydays and too much liquor resulted in a sorry state of affairs. Fortunately, that didn't happen too often. We never had that experience, thank goodness.

However, there were times when people were actually chained or tied to the house in order to enforce the restrictions. As far as discipline was concerned, other parents would administer it as needed to anyone who was wrong, unfair, mean or brought embarrassment to the family or neighborhood area. If one went home and complained that they had received a slap from someone you were immediately slapped or spanked again, THEN you were asked, WHY? You must have been doing something wrong in the eyes of an adult or else you would not have received the punishment.

It is difficult to determine whether our parents copied the river or our parents influenced the river, for the river was an unforgiving disciplinarian and allowed no room for error or mistakes. I guess it was the parents who were more forgiving and perhaps more loving than the river. Another incident my father reacted to was an injustice that occurred when a teacher had struck a young girl across the back raising quite a welt, using a fourteen inch ruler, the extra thick kind. My sister came home and told my father and he apparently saw the parents of the child, saw the welt, heard the story, and marched over a mile to the town hall to see his 'influential buddies'. The next day the teacher was transferred to another school. She had a reputation for being "just mean" as my brother would say. I believe we were the only ones who knew what Pop had done.

Before the area behind the breakwater was filled, it extended for over a quarter a mile. I remember a neighbor, Mrs. H and her crabbing, which she did by setting bait attached to lines, or by walking along scooping crabs for dinner. They, the H's, lived above our house on the hill that overlooked our home and had a view of the river and the tracks. They commanded a view of everything so knew everything. You couldn't escape Mrs. H's view of all. She was quite vigilant about neighborhood activities. We learned to walk and run in an area out of her view. A stairway went up from the main street over the cliff to her home, it had a good sized porch on which she would sit or stand.

When we first made her acquaintance it was in response to a very loud yelling of 'oil, oil', a hesitation and then again, 'oil, oil' . . . Who in their right mind would advertise for oil in that manner? This went on for more than a week until we met her son. His name was EARL. She had a slight accent and the name came out 'oil.' She was very industrious woman and went fishing and crabbing. She would also send her son out to catch fish . . .

I remember taking him with us and fishing for tomcods and without question he would always catch more than we did . . . and in our boat! We went to the woolen mill dock when the season was right and the tomcods were running. We never did out fish that young man. His nickname was Popeye. He got his name from trying to lift the rear end of a Baby Austin. Of course, he suffered the rest of his life from a hernia, or so he said.

If anyone larger than he pushed him or bumped him he always cried that the hernia pained him . . . He wore a belt to keep his navel from protruding, which they claimed was a hernia. Of course, he could jump, swim, run like the dickens, fall, roll and any number of athletic activities, but bump him or push him and there was an alarm sent that you might have injured his hernia. I never understood the situation, but I never got into any brawls or altercations with Popeye. I enjoyed his company and he was humorous. His mother was quite a lady. She was the one who taught him how to fish and do all the important river front activities that were needed for survival. The rest of us were good watchers and listeners and became rather adept at some of the survival skills she taught her son.

# CHAPTER VII

## NEIGHBORHOOD WATCHERS

She wasn't the only person who taught us various skills. Everyone in the neighborhood was a teacher. Where did you learn that we were asked by many neighbors. Mrs. or Mr. So-In-So. Okay, must be true. We respected older people and their opinions and enjoyed gleaning their knowledge. The final judgment as to whether or not this knowledge was useful was from our parents. Sometimes they learned as well! Anyway, back to Mrs. H . . . She was quite the spectacle wearing her dress and rolled stockings and walking on the breakwater in large high top shoes. Popeye was the only son that I can recall, I think he had a couple of sisters, one older and one younger. They were nice and would come down over the three foot wall that separated our house lot from theirs. We owned ours, but they rented the bottom floor of a three family house.

Another memorable character along with Mrs. H was "Jimmy the Beggar". He lived adjacent to the tracks in a small house which had a walk out cellar opening to the path we traveled to get to and from the tracks and river. He was quite a character and a nice man although at times we thought he was pretty strange. We respected him but kept our distance and I can't recall if it was in awe or fear or a combination of the two. I recall that the hill and path past his house was very steep, about a sixty degree angle, and we would actually run up and down that slope. Usually it was a race to see who would get to the swimming area first so not to be 'IT'. He actually would tell us how to do various tasks, from planting a garden, collecting bottles for money, trapping eels, tying lines. You needed to take time to listen. He was a moody man and sometimes he would chase us away for no apparent reason. Later we would find out that someone had done something to Jimmy for which we paid the penalty.

There were a few other women who would come crabbing, I think Mrs. J, and Mrs. D made an effort to get food from the river. I often wonder how many laughs we gave them as we scampered to and from our destinations and clandestine meetings. We thought we were getting away with things, when in reality everything we did was recorded in the eyes of loving guardians from our neighborhood. Mrs. J was especially nice and her son was a few years older than I was but equally as nice as his mother. I liked him and trusted him, but as I said, he was a little older and out of our age group. I do recall that he was a very powerfully built young man and not one with whom one would want to have a physical disagreement! My vision of him is that of splitting wood for the stove. I recalled my own days of splitting kindling and the likes and can identify with that vision.

While living in that area, our father worked a rotating shift. One night he came home and was suddenly in agony. He told my mother to hit him in the head with the axe to render him unconscious because the pain was so severe. I guess stomach ulcers had ruptured or his appendix had burst. I forget which for he experienced both at different times. Anyway, that caused his agony AND he was in the hospital for several weeks and there was no income. Cash was short and food was limited (thank goodness for the neighbors). We had to cut wood for the kitchen stove, so one of my tasks was to split wood into kindling size. One day a bill collector came and my mother didn't have the ten cents or whatever. Being in arrears, for probably an insurance policy, she told the collector that her husband was in the hospital and she had no money. He became belligerent and said he wasn't leaving till she paid what she owed. I don't recall clearly if my mother pushed him back from the rear door or what, for she was close to tears and kept telling him to leave. At this point I was behind him, with the axe raised, checking the over head branches for clearance, and asked, "Should I hit him, Ma?" He turned to see me poised with the blade ready to split a 'kindling brain'.

My mother ran to me yelling "No, No, Dan, No!" My mother held me back from chasing him. He lost his hat going around the corner of the house and never came back to get it. Nice hat too. It isn't difficult to imagine a wife beater getting bludgeoned by sons or daughters when coming to the defense of a battered mother or even a father.

Returning to Mrs. J and her son; I lost track of them and finally after sixty-five plus years found out what happened to the son. They lived in sort of a commune with three or four houses; Jimmy's, Mrs. J's, and Mrs. D's, plus one other, the name of whom I can't recall.

We knew that getting food for the family was an important part of life, therefore we started hunting at an early age. We went for squirrels, rabbits, pheasants, or whatever we could bring home. I recall my mother chasing a pheasant that had ventured a little too close to the house; she got it with a broom. That's when I found out that they are plucked just like a chicken. I wasn't a bad shot, but my brother was a fantastic shot. In later years I was better with handguns, but he was a master with a rifle. We would go after small game and bring back whatever we could.

One of the areas I mentioned was the breakwaters In years past there was an entirely different means of getting the game once it was shot. There were ducks in the winter season when there was slushy ice present. We had no dogs so if you shot a duck or goose you had to figure that the wave action would wash it toward you allowing you to pick it up. Prior to the storm ('38 hurricane) there were nowhere near as many cormorants, opossums or cardinals that we could remember. What strange evolutionary changes are stimulated by storms. Also, it was close to ten years before the return of crabs in any quantity.

I look back at that storm as the turning point of the "warming trend" being experienced currently, including the ozone hole and all it represents. After studying Geology, Ecology, Climatology and Pleistocene Geology, it is clear that this is a cyclical activity and there is nothing anyone can do to alter its course; perhaps they can slow it but nothing will alter its course.

Our uncle was a super marksman and went hunting on his father's land but when he exited, he was arrested for illegal hunting. These actions appear to show the idiocy of the local law enforcement agents at that time. All these people were trying to do was to hunt for food for their table. He later served in the Army from Africa to the Alps as a BAR man We also hunted but we would walk along the tracks to get to a hunting area; one place we hunted was near the old milk house. Do you know what a milk house is? It's a train stop where the farmers would unload their milk cans and pick up the empties that the milk train left. All of the cans had markings identifying the owners.

There was a wooded area near the milk house that was fairly good for hunting. I don't know who owned this land but it didn't make any difference because everyone worked together to help each other. No one was destructive. If we climbed over a stone wall and a rock fell, we picked it up and replaced it. If it happened and we saw another down, we'd replace that one as well. Don't get the idea we were angels we were not. We were mischievous at times but never deliberately destructive. On one trip to this area, a huge gull flew over and I thought, why not? They're just like chicken. I'll shoot it, clean it and say it was a pheasant or something similar. There was a quivering of the bird in flight, then it just continued to soar looking for its lunch. To say I was shocked would be an understatement. It was then I realized that some birds have many layers of feathers that act like armor so that you must be close enough to have a bullet penetrate the bird. Never again did I try that sort of stupid act.

We had a teacher named Miss Kilroy. She was probably one of the most unique teachers anyone could experience. She may very well have been the impetuous for the success of many students who otherwise would have been deemed average. She was the principal/teacher at the school we attended. She had about sixty students in a combined fifth and sixth grades. Can you imagine a teacher today trying to handle sixty students and keep them interested and studying?

I have mentioned this teacher before in other articles; how she probably knew more about our antics than any other person. She did have a great deal of respect for our privacy and our need to explore. She is also one who recognized my abilities and shortcomings early on and never let me get away with slovenly work. She praised me a few times but made me pay the penalty at other times. She probably knew where we usually were but I think that is because of a little maid named 'Frannie' whom I have mentioned in other writings.

Miss Kilroy had a leather strop with which she'd administer discipline. It was hidden by the students behind the picture of George Washington. Another time there was an eraser throwing contest between a couple of the boys and one was thrown just as Miss Kilroy came into the room. This struck her in the head leaving an undeniable white mark. This may have been when she noticed the strop had disappeared. These stories were relayed to me by my brother who was one year behind me in school. Teacher comparison showed that he was undeniably a better student. The teachers always breathed a sigh of relief when he showed such promise after struggling with me.

# Chapter VIII

## TEMPORARY REPRIEVE FROM THE RIVER

We used to play King of the Hill and Red Rover at various times and in various places. Anytime there was a higher bit of ground such as a slope or a dirt-pile, someone would stand on top and inevitably the game would start. At times there was no intention to begin the game but one would merely get on the peak to get a better view only to find himself rolling down unexpectedly and that would automatically start the game. I never recall anyone being the winner. It was just fun to play.

Along the rivers, between the east and west sides, there was a turntable for reversing engines It was called a Roundhouse. After the '38 hurricane it wasn't being used very much. The entire region including Water Street, Bath Street, the lower part of West Thames or West Main Street was flooded, causing a great deal of damage. There were two train tunnels, one led to the roundhouse. I believe there was another roundhouse in the Greenville area but on our side of the river it was too high to be flooded so it was free of debris.

After walking the rails the day after the hurricane, it was time to see what else had happened. When we were allowed to cross the bridge into the town, we did so. We then immediately detoured to the other railroad. We walked through the tunnel that led to the roundhouse. There was a little dispute about the exact location of that roundhouse. We knew there was a repair building adjacent to the Shetucket River. It was supposed that that was the roundtable. Another concept was that it was on Hollyhock Island.

The tunnel was not in good condition. Boxes, branches, limbs, mud and a variety of debris was along the tracks and in the tunnel. It gave us a chill, a frightening feeling as we approached it thinking it might collapse. I recall the trepidation with which we maneuvered into the tunnel. The bridge to Hollyhock Island was cluttered with branches and timbers. It seemed as though the river had retaliated by the storms urging. Hollyhock Island was the site of the main dockage in the harbor, especially the coal unloading and Island storage facility.

View from Hollyhock Island, near the back of the Episcopal
Church on Washington Street

The Greenville roundhouse still exists and is where Shetucket Plumbing has their warehouse. After visiting the roundhouse, I began to think that they should have a public tour once or twice a year so people can see the amazing construction. You could even charge admission, at least enough to pay the electric bill. They would also need floodlights to illuminate the bracing at its location on North Main Street, Norwich, Ct.

Gardens were an assigned responsibility bestowed upon us by our parents. We'd had gardens most of our short lives. Pop managed to locate a farm or two that let him use a piece of land to plant a garden. In return the farmer wanted a percentage of the crops. One of the first times we planted a crop of vegetables on a farm in Yantic, Pop had us do the weeding and hilling. The farmer made use of us as well especially my brother who got paid fifty cents for his work one summer. What I recall mostly is the farm that was between six to seven miles from our house and the river. We would walk to weed, hill, and spray or dust. Dusting was done with a mechanical contraption with a rotating crank that created a draught which blew the powder out from the storage bin. A long three-plus foot tubing was attached to a fluted arrangement that spread the dust onto the potato plants. This was to rid the plants of the potatoes bugs that were prevalent. This was the only way to get rid of them at that time. Or, we could pick them off and place them into jars or cans with kerosene but this didn't get rid of the eggs or larvae. We used 'Arsenic of Lead' as the control and breathed it in even though we used handkerchiefs We miraculously avoided being poisoned or biting the dust.

In retrospect, we were hired out and never knew it. Our thoughts were that we were helping do a good thing, plus harvesting our own food. We'd walk down to the farm, spend the day, and walk back. I don't recall taking a lunch on many of these outings. Occasionally, the farmer's wife would drive us back. She was a petite woman and very much on the ball. She was not appreciated as much as she should have been. There were times when we'd stay over upstairs in a spare room. I have forgotten how many acres were planted at that farm, and I mentioned this to my brother. We tried to figure out what happened to all the veggies and potatoes. I recall a few one hundred pound. bags being in the cellar of our home, but don't recall what happened to the rest. Of course, my mother had sisters and friends who needed help so we are sure that they each got a bushel of potatoes. Also my father's sisters received another bushel or two and I'm sure the farmer got his share and then some, but what of the other sacks? We finally figured that he must have sold rest and also that the farmers probably paid Pop for our services. When they gave us fifty cents, it was a tip in addition to the salary earned.

During the war, we joined the FFA (Future Farmers of America). It was 1943 Good bye river and its pleasures. We were sent to a tomato farm and apple orchard. We worked sixty hours a week all summer for nine dollars per week in order to help the war effort. Seven dollars went to the YMCA for food and lodging so we ended up with only two dollars per week. 'T was the war effort. We did our part. They had canvass cots set up on the gym floor should you erroneously think we had rooms. That's only three and one third cents per hour.

I found the certificate that they gave us, entitled, U.S. CROP CORPS CERTIFICATE OF SERVICE awarded to__(name)_____ For patriotic service on a farm or in a food processing factory, signed by Chester Davis, WAR FOOD ADMINISTRATOR, Paul M. Nutt, CHAIRMAN, WAR MANPOWER COMMISSION, and E. Woodward, STATE DIRECTOR OF AGRICULTURAL EXTENSION. At three and a third cents an hour, would this be considered unfair labor practice? Other people were suing for lesser reasons but if I can prove even an estimate of the hours we put in, do you think we could get the minimum wage reimbursements? Good luck!

The railroad ties were stacked after re-tamping and replacement. The dredging of the river by dumping the sand and mud into this area extended the cove shoreline by several hundred feet and may have added as much as five to ten acres of land to the south of the lumberyard but reduced our cove by the same acreage. The distance was over eleven hundred feet of fill (photo pg. 31). One can follow the breakwater up and on the left there is a slight jog going to the left. That was the end of the dockage at the lumber yard. The photos on pgs. 32 and 83 shows the cove and breakwater as it currently looks during winter as you look north.

Polish was a language that was prevalent in our neighborhood. There was also French-Canadian and some Portuguese so learning to swear in another language was not difficult. Some Yiddish crept in on occasion as well. If you slipped and swore in another language, it never seemed as bad so it was sort of accepted, but once our parents learned what it meant, we were in trouble. Several older people encouraged us to learn the languages. One person was Johnny's mother. Johnny would teach us certain phrases which we freely used amongst ourselves. Hello, How are you, Thank you, and some other words. On one occasion Johnny told me exactly how to address his mother so as to be the recipient of the mouth watering potato pancakes she was making. The whole yard smelled of good food. I complied as I was standing in the kitchen thinking I was doing a good job. After speaking the phrase she hauled off and slapped me with no lack of force. I looked very startled as Johnny was laughing and running out the kitchen door. A few weeks later he tried it again but I reminded him of the last time and said NO! He assured me that this time would be different and crossed his heart and "hoped to die". Well, naturally, with such a sacred oath I stood in the kitchen and quoted carefully what I had been coached to say. Upon completion she smiled and in broken English said, "Ah, you learn Polish! My son, he teach you Polish?" At that I beamed suspecting that I had done a good job. Her son had indeed instructed me whereupon she hit him with a closed fist, knocking him down under the table. She then turned to me and said, "You want to learn Polish, you come see me. I teach you Polish." Johnny never again told us any improper things to say. She may have spoken broken English, but she certainly wasn't an ignorant woman and she became a giant in my eyes in spite of her four foot eleven inch, one hundred ten pound frame.

In addition to becoming 'limited linguists' we took excursions to the woods up near Johnny and Charles' house, Charlie was the brains in the neighborhood and didn't really participate much with the rest of us. Later he became a physicist but he died prematurely. I have started a separate tribute to Charlie and his contributions to society. Past the adjacent lots behind our home, Johnny had a wooden hut or hide-away where we learned to smoke and roll our own cigarettes. We'd usually start from the lots if we were not on the river, and follow the many trails. One such trip started at the open lot behind our home, and traveled over the old logging trails/roads to wild adventures of the early explorers and trappers. Some trails were old stage coach lines we discovered by accompanying our parents on Sunday afternoon forays. We were 'allowed' to accompany our parents on Sundays if it was not inclement weather. We'd walk the old trails or logging roads and were introduced to the stage coach roads that ran all the way to Stonington through Poquetanuck, Ledyard and North Stonington. We never walked the whole trail but did find the old road in many places, even the places where it would curve to and from the new road. Once it was pointed out to you, it became quite obvious. We'd hike to Poquetanuck, then around to the highway and back home again. There were all kinds of connecting trails, logging roads or old drives to abandoned farms that most people will never see.

While we were on the overgrown rutted trail we discovered a field of white birch trees that were ideal for climbing, swinging and bending. Some of the guys were later able to travel fifty to a hundred feet from tree to tree without touching the ground. When we read Frost's poem, "When Two Roads Diverge In A Woods" in later years there was an instant identification with the poem. Black birch trees were a challenge for shimmying up. This increased our arm and leg strength for all sorts of other activities. Sunday walks with our parents were adventurous as well as educational. I was always impressed by my mother's knowledge of herbs and plants. Years later I found out that her mother, my grandmother, had been brought up by her grandmother who was an herbalist and mid-wife in Austria. Now I wish I had paid more attention then. My mother was full of surprises.

Poquetanuck, where we'd hike down to the upper end of the Draw Bridge Cove, actually the Poquetanuck Cove, we would dam the narrow neck on the land side of the road and trap shad when they were running, take them to Budnick's, Fish Market and sell them for whatever the going price was that day. Our difficulty was carrying or transporting the fish about four miles to the store. Some kids had parents who would pick them up in a car or truck but we had no such transportation.

Poquetanuck Cove where we trapped fish

The advent of bicycles helped us but till then walking was necessary. I recall once when we walked with over half a bushel of fish all the way to the West side. We had wrapped the wire handles with cloth or paper and used a stick through the handles to save our hands. It was a struggle, and when we got there, they didn't want the fish. We left them anyway and went home rather dejected. In retrospect, we should have brought them home with us, but we were exhausted after such an arduous trip. Remember that we were only ten, or the oldest twelve. Two kids carried over half a bushel of fish that far. It showed determination. We should have brought them home for I'm pretty sure that they sold them after we left. We found out later about the various types of business transactions that went on there.

We passed the Strand Theater on our return and I rather think that we had planned to go there with the money we expected to receive. The movies were only a dime or eleven cents with the usual serial adventures that kept you returning. They also gave away set of dishes for an extra four or five cents. You returned so that you could obtain the entire set. How much they really were worth I really don't recall but I recently read where a complete set of that vintage sold for several thousand dollars. It was a good investment for those who saved them. We'd go to the movies if we could find the money. We managed this by looking for soda bottles or bleach bottles. Bleach bottles brought in five cents so they were scarce but much sought after. It kept the neighborhood pretty clear of debris.

My cousins would go to the movies and sit through two if not three showings. Our parents always mentioned one show only as we left. Cartoons came first in the beginning, so we'd always sit through that twice. Then they changed the venue so that serials came first, which we would sit through twice. Then it became a question of what was going to be shown first. The news reels, "the Eyes and Ears of the World," Pathé News. Occasionally we'd play on the emotions of my mother and persuade her to let us stay longer and she'd allow us as long as we were home no later than six.

When coming out of the movie we were often intercepted by mothers wanting to know if their children were still there or even where they were sitting. Some of the kids changed their seats in order to move closer to the front for a better seat after it was vacated. I never really liked the closer seats, because sitting in or towards the back allowed us to see all that went on. On occasion, we witnessed seeing a parent walking toward the front, stopping and pointing saying, 'YOU! YOU COME OUT NOW!'. The kid would rise and inevitably walk to the aisle opposite from where the parent would be standing!

Our first movie that I can recall was "CAPTAIN BLOOD". It played at the Palace which was a treat by our father who liked the historical type movie. I may have fallen asleep for I cannot recall the action except for a battle scene on a ship. That is about all. On another occasion we were at a Western with our father and Buck Jones or Tom Mix had someone sneaking up behind him and my brother yelled out in a very loud voice, 'LOOK OUT, BEHIND YOU'. The audience responded with laughter but it shows the intensity one gets being personally involved in action movies.

Crazy Louie had a salvage store where you could buy all sorts of things. He'd sit outside on the sidewalk and talk with you. One of his eyes popped out or protruded giving him a really weird look, but as my mother would say, you can't judge a book by its cover. If he hadn't seen us for awhile, he'd always ask our names to identify us with the proper family. He apparently knew our parents and I strongly suspect would report to them if they happened to walk past. Next to his store was a

'Brandywine' package store. They were nice as well, but we didn't see them as often. I don't recall if they sold soda as well as other beverages. Bath Street was an interesting market place.

Our excursions were not always at the river. Before or after a swim, we'd try other activities which were usually within a few miles of the docks. One location was the lot behind our house. Now it is so overgrown that I didn't recognize it as I drove up Rogers Avenue. If we didn't attend movies or go out in the boat, we'd have trips to the woods and lots. One of the areas we visited had outcroppings of rock or cliffs that had a path running diagonally up to the highlands, the blueberry lot, and the birches area which was the old stage line. At the base of the cliff there was a swampy region with a small stream, ideal for building dams. It was also excellent for playing cowboys depending on which movie we had recently seen.

The outcropping opposite this was nearer to our home and adjacent to the lot. We could see it from our upstairs window. In that outcropping there was a wedge of rock that was rectangular and about fifteen feet long, two feet wide, it was a separated area adjacent to the cliff. There was a two to three foot natural trench that was an ideal fort commanding a view of the field, the swamp and the road (logging) between the field and swamp area. We traveled that road periodically. It eventually connected with Talmund Street and the East Side.

It went past a farm that had a nice apple tree. There were reported stories of having been shot at with rock-salt. This enhanced our respect for the farmer who lived there. The road then became an improved secondary road. There was also a branch of that road that went on to become the part of the stage line in the highlands. The farmer frowned on us using this road even though it was a ROW (Right Of Way). We didn't understand that until years later so we traveled there with great trepidation.

One year above this farm near the blueberry lot we were having a noisy game with cap pistols. Suddenly we heard sirens and looked down to the old road which was really more of a grassy trail and saw a couple of police cars. The police got out with their guns drawn and crouched down next to their cars while we fired our caps. In reality, some of the kids never saw or heard the police until we called their attention to their presence. Eventually they drove away We left thinking they might be driving around to the other side to cut us off and arrest us for trespassing so we dispersed to the various trails we knew and scattered home. I can just hear the response from our parents if we had told them about the situation, Their reply would be "You Did What? Suppose they shot back at you?" We did tell them casually several weeks later after someone had leaked the information but by that time it was a watered down version.

A challenge was extended for me to climb the most vertical and highest portion of the cliff near the swampy area. I started up, reached the crack-like ridge in about the middle. We knew that it was about four inches wide in some places and had a small alcove area that may have been ten inches high and two feet long along the ridge crack. The face of the cliff went up almost vertically to the top. I reached into the ridge with my fingers with my arm fully extended. I then inched up, got a toe hold, edged up, put my hand further into the crack for a better grip and lifted myself. Next I got my right hand up to the crack pulled, and got a better toe hold. Then I raised my body up and reached in further with my left hand. I felt something move at the same time that I brought my eyes to the level to see several snakes in the small opening. I let out a scream and dropped ten to fifteen feet to the swamp edge while two snakes landed simultaneously with me. Such an unexpected happening with the slithering copperheads set off an alarm to the rest of the crew that all the cliffs were heavily infested with copperheads. We eventually realized they were not copperheads but rather garter snakes. It certainly curtailed our rock climbing activities. Usually those were late fall, winter and early spring activities, for the river was our goddess during the late spring, summer and early fall. Of course, there were a few times when we went to the woods for specific purposes in the summer.

One purpose was for blueberries. The blueberry lot was known far and wide as one of the best; it had many of high bush berries from which we'd collect fruit and our moms would bake blueberry pies. No one has ever surpassed my mother's pies for taste, texture, crust, flavor, and overall excellence. Our favorite bush was near the path by the cliffs. It was also where we'd find an occasional blacksnake resting in the branches, either eating or waiting for a bird. We never disturbed it because we were taught that blacksnakes were good to have around. They ate mice and other rodents, as well as birds. My first encounter with a blacksnake was an eye to eye startling introduction. I then backed off and went to another bush There was plenty of room for both of us, but as I approached the new bush the memory of the snake caused me to be careful because another snake might be resting in the branches. By the time we got back to the first bush the snake was gone and so were the berries. That was one of the few trails or paths where we usually walked. Otherwise, we ran or jogged, as they would say today, long before they coined the word.

# CHAPTER IX

## BACK TO THE RIVER:

## THE ELTO ACE AND OTHER ACTIVITIES

THE MOTOR! I have to put that in caps, a new MOTOR. an Elto Ace. One point eight horsepower. We could be at the cove in a half hour. The drawbridge in less than an hour and with the wind, current and tide favorable we could be in New London in three hours. It took us awhile, but we finally learned to operate and care for the motor. We learned how to go into shallows and avoid the prop hitting the sand or mud which would kick up a cloud of black, grey, or brown water.

On our first adventure the motor was running perfectly, but the prop didn't turn which resulted in a racing engine but no movement. A thanks be to God that we had the oars. We had hit a partially sunken object and had broken a shear pin. After that we always had extra shear pins with us and learned that eight penny nails could be used at times or coat hanger wire (the thick ones) as substitutes in an emergency. It did not take much strain on the early engines to pop those pins. It seems that almost anything with slight resistance would cause the pins to shear. I recall bending nails or heavy wire to accommodate the need. We'd use whatever would fit into the slot, replace the prop and be on our way.

We could run all day using a two gallon can of mixed gas and have some left over at the end of the day. Gas was between fifteen to

seventeen cents a gallon plus the cost of the oil, so for about fifty cents
we could go to New London and back and still have enough left to
cruise around. I think the engine tank had about a pint capacity. The
starter rope would occasionally get frayed or the knot would break, so
we'd just tie a new knot and be on our way until the rope got too short.
Clothes line made a good starter line to start the motor as long as it
wasn't the cotton type. We had no reverse so had to slow down and spin
the engine around to reverse its direction. It was tricky, but functional.
We had to be extra careful at first going into the shallow water with the
engine until we learned to tilt the engine up. We did learn though. We
towed one or two other boats as we traveled the river. Our anchor line
was quite long, but we also had mooring lines plus an extra anchor,
food, fishing lines, and crabbing lines which were usually the same
as the fishing lines. I can't recall any poles other than sticks and crab
net but not a fishing net. I can't remember a fish net ever being used.
Sometimes we'd be on our way home and another boat (scow) would
be going in our direction so we'd come along side, lash gunnels to
gunnels, so we could talk and compare stories of "You shudda seen the
one that we almost got!" Or, "The crab was two hands tip to tip but we
missed it." We never really measured them, since we could pretty well
eyeball the legal size. Of course the water magnified the size. One of
the definite advantages of having a motor was the time it would take to
transport fish or crabs to the fish market. Each time we went, other kids
had gotten there first so we eventually gave up.

One of our longer trips using the motor was going to the New
London Light. We passed the sub base and under the car and
railroad bridges. They didn't need to open the bridges for us but we
were awed by those girders! Look at those rivets, gears and counter
weights. Awesome! We passed the Electric Boat Company, the light
and then back. On the return trip there was a twenty eight foot whale
boat with each thwart occupied by an oarsman. The Navy boys were
rowing and said they needed a tow which we were willing to do. They
jokingly tossed us a line. We were making it fast to our re-enforced
stern, but they prevailed upon us to let the line go. They were standing
and screaming for us to release the line. They were afraid we'd have
pulled out the stern. They thanked us and then breathed a sigh of
relief. We investigated all sorts of places on the river, but our area
of concentration was from the drawbridge north to the G & E ( Gas
and Electric) plant, the harbor to Trading Cove and of course, the
breakwaters.

One of our walking tours was to a sand or gravel bank along the
tracks. At the top was a large oak tree with a huge branch running

parallel to the tracks. It was where someone had tied a hawser. The branch was ten to fifteen feet above the bank which meant we could swing out over the tracks at a safe height. The arc of swing went almost to the edge of the river and many times we entertained the thought as to whether we'd reach the water if we let go. We knew the water was too shallow, within the breakwater mud flat area, but we always wondered. Good thing we never tried. We'd never have made it! The swing area was opposite the woolen mill and on one occasion a couple of guys swung out through the smoke of the engine never thinking that they would be going through soot and sparks. I wonder what the fireman and engineer thought of that little escapade? I think the swing disappeared. It could have been the hurricane that decimated that portion of our playground but I'm not sure.

There were water towers that had ladders on them, but we never climbed them even though we wanted to see the view or at least have the satisfaction of being able to say we had done it. However, there were two that we did climb. One was the spherical gas storage tank that was twenty to thirty feet in diameter located just behind the school. The other water tower was in Ledyard or Poquetanuck, near a melon patch that we occasionally visited especially after we got our own bicycles.

School with gas storage sphere in rear

On one excursion to this patch I remember finding a large melon and putting it into the basket on the front of the bike I then headed down a dirt road where there was a slight curve. My tire skidded in a little sand and with the added weight on the front it caused the bike, me, and the melon to end up in a ditch. Fortunately, no damage was done. With bikes we had more distance we could travel and on a few nights in the summer we'd leave on route 32, go to New London over the bridge into Groton, and return northerly on route 12 which had more curves than any road in the area. It was always dark when we headed north and the lights they had on bikes at that time were dependant on batteries which inevitably would jar loose and out would go the light. This road had 19 curves within the 5 miles we traveled that they took out when they rebuilt the road. Some people claimed that the road had fifty curves within a distance of twelve miles.

I never saw a bike light that illuminated sufficiently to be really safe and useful. The guys who had generators still had problems because of the bouncing and jamming of their bike lights. Flats were another problem. Some of the kids had balloon tires and the rest had the narrow tires. Pumps were scarce but it was not a major problem since most service stations would supply air and repaired the flats either with us or sometimes for us. We learned to carry patch cans after we had a few long walks home practically carrying a bike. On these long night forays we were fairly lucky and seldom had a flat. Occasionally some of the guys would try to leave you in the dust but usually we caught up. The difficult part of these late night activities with poor lights was going downhill at a rapid speed only to encounter a curve and a sudden swerve to avoid going off the road. This was before there were lines on the roads. When they finally painted the fog lines on the edge of the roads, it was a huge help to us.

Another activity that was rarely a problem was drinking water. We knew where the springs were to get water but I don't recall carrying water or stopping for a drink except on long trips. The first thing you did when you got home was to drink a glass or two of water, then it would be supper time. You ate less because you had filled up on water. No wonder we seldom were overweight.

One winter it was very cold either, 1938 or 1939. My uncle lived over the water in a shack on pilings with no insulation. He came to stay with us for a few months. That was one thing about the river; as welcoming as it might seem, there were times when it drove you away. If your house was on pilings there could be a foot of ice underneath and the chance of shifting ice could take your house down without any warning. This was a scary feeling especially with the tidal surges. The ice could move and take everything with it. Kelly's boat, a one hundred footer, had cribbing along the bank and was left on the land and appeared stable.

In any event, my uncle came to live with us and shared the room with the boys. He had a day bed in one corner. We were on the third floor, and with him came Hop Leg. This character was created by him several years before when we all lived in a boarding house. The cellar had a dirt floor and one corner had a very small window that admitted a limited amount of light. Hop Leg consisted of a leg and a head and would thump around making noises that my uncle would imitate either by thumping on something while he told of Hop Leg's adventures looking for the rest of his body. There were times when we'd hear the thump but didn't see our uncle strike anything. I know he must have had some set-up to make the noise but for little kids it was a mystery. These stories continued during the winter and many times one could hear the leg thump up the stairs while our uncle chased Hop Leg and yelled that it could not go up stairs; because there were nice kids up there and a tussle occurred where he would wrestle Hop Leg down the stairs. While this was going on he would yell to us not to be frightened, he was taking him down the stairs. We never saw any of this for we were hidden beneath the covers in fear.

I only learned later that my mother apparently was quite an athlete in her youth. She was a runner and jumper as well as the recipient of several ribbons for track. Her biggest achievement was her ice skating abilities. She was quite adept on the blades and was purposed to have cleared five to seven barrels in one jump. We were told by other people than my family things such as, "You should have seen your mother on skates; she could skate so well". When asked about it she merely said yes, I did that, and that was the end of it.

I wanted a pair of figure skates so that I could try to imitate Sonja Henie and other skaters. But alas, I fell, got up and tried again. It was embarrassing to have anything other than hockey skates if you were a boy so figure skates were out. As I was trying spins one day someone came and showed me a way of doing jumps and splits but kindly said that I should have figure skates because of the different shape of the blades. About that time the hockey game started so no more lessons. We would stuff magazines into our stockings to prevent getting our shins bashed. I still have scars attesting to the roughness of sticks and skates. I don't recall anyone going home to get bandaged but if they did they'd be back in half an hour ready to go again. Now they'd rush you to a hospital to get x-rayed.

# UNCLE GUS' HOMESTEAD ON THE RIVER!

## NOTICE THE ICE COVERED RIVER! TO THE LEFT OF THE FLAG IS THE THERMOS COMPANY AND OUR COVE

In addition to swimming, boating, running and other sports that were of interest to young people, in the winter we had hockey. Our father decided to buy hockey skates for the boys and figure skates for Hadie and Mom. Of course, my mom could skate circles around us if she wanted to but she was a cautious mom. We were not allowed to go on the river but there was a small pond where all the kids managed to congregate. If it snowed, we all showed up with shovels and cleared the pond. We also made pathways for tag games or Fox and Geese, a game that is played equally as well in a field of hay or grass. I still keep one Fox and Geese area constantly cut to the delight of my grandchildren.

Fox and geese game area

With the advent of playgrounds came the increased interest in baseball, softball, volleyball, horseshoes, swinging and climbing the swings. These were an outgrowth from our sandlot games. I don't recall if they were organized, but frequently sandlot games occurred spontaneously. On many occasions, while walking to the city or home, past an ongoing game, someone would shout that another player was needed. Your mission would then change according to the current need, whether quarterback, catcher, or net stretcher for volleyball. After we broke a window in the yellow house near the park, we had to reverse our home plate in order to hit the ball toward the road at the end of the park.

Once in awhile we'd be invited to other city areas to play. Some areas had regular pick-up games every Sunday in places such as the Norwich-Town green. People would travel there to watch either baseball or football. Years later, the entire high-school senior football team responded to a challenge but were severely beaten by school chums who couldn't go out for the team due to after school work schedules. Also, several had been prevented from playing on the team because some "official's" son had priority. This went on for several Sundays, the official team getting trounced by the put-together-on-the-spot team. When the coach discovered this activity he was embarrassed and he put a stop to it. No longer were the players able to participate in such activities for fear of injury to a valuable player. Another part of the embarrassment was that several of the put-together-on-the-spot players had been cut from playing on the official team in order to make room for the more intelligent and select few. This began after spring practice and went on into the summer. I recall that there was a newspaper article that caught the coach's attention. This brought about much heckling from the sidelines during August practice games. The best players never went out for the team since they had commitments to a job as well as the need for academic study time. Many of these better players didn't have the status that seemed to be required. Knowing several of these people, it was quite evident that they had the brain power to attend college, but didn't. The reason? No one at that time helped the unknowns, or persons from that other societal group without status. The so called guidance people were very protective of keeping the scholarships and financial aid programs for the un-needy. A sad state of affairs.

I mentioned the river freezing over and recall skating a few times near the breakwater in the cove, but can't recall going outside the cove area. Of course, we'd try ice fishing but our techniques were pretty lousy. We did cut holes in the ice and use long poles with three to five pronged barbs to probe the mud for eels but our fishing skills in the winter were poor. The breakwaters were too slippery when they had a glaze of ice over them and the rough edges along the shores were sometimes too difficult to get over in order to get on to the ice. It was as though the river was telling us that she was too dangerous and to stay away until she was in a better mood. That didn't mean we wouldn't walk beside her to experience the wind and beauty of the ice and reminisce about the past summer's excursions and the 'big ones' we ALMOST caught.

This is why we stayed off breakwaters in winter

Our cove today from a boat mooring area

The rock for weighing down the diving board

Once flat topped is now irregular due to ice and water movement

From an island looking north, woolen mill is seen in distance

The woolen mill is currently in a sad state

The pilings where the old dock was. Notice the close proximity
to the thermos factory—they had great views!

One year one of our friends received a pair of skis which we all
tried to maneuver in the back lots. A few experience skiers had made
a run and even build a ski jump. I tried desperately to make the turns
and control the skis but it didn't turn out that way. They controlled
me. I did make it down the slope once, made the jump and continued
down to the old road. It was the only time that I can recall being
successful. I was thrilled but no matter how many times I tried it after
that, no such luck. My feet would slip out, the ski would get caught, the
nose of the ski went under the snow, my foot would turn but the ski
stayed straight or would go where ever it wanted and ice built up under
my shoe. I was a disaster! That one successful run kept coming back in
my memory and the wonderful feeling of accomplishment, that thrill,
that desire to again experience the feeling of triumph enticed me
to go back and try again and again. The last time I tried, most of the
snow had disappeared and I stopped short on the grassy area six feet
shy of the rest of the snow trail. I picked up the skis and headed home
thinking of the boat as being a better form of transportation for me.

The river was calling; a loud call and clear call which cannot be
denied ( Mansfield's "Sea Fever") making me believe she was more fun
than the slopes or the woods for we were akin to her. Eventually I did
learn to ski but it was forty years later!

Another fun time was when we'd pick up some empty oil cans, step
on them, bang the edges of the cans to our instep with a stone or rock
and go clippity-clopping down the street making a racket. This did not

work well with Keds. You needed a sole for attachment. Sometimes you didn't want to take the cans off if you had a tight fit and I learned that it didn't work well if you removed your shoes without taking the cans off since you couldn't get your shoes back on. In the winter we tried it a few times but it wasn't the same. Besides, if there was ice, there was uncontrolled skidding. Overshoes were not good for attachments. I wonder, does anyone use overshoes anymore? Or 'arctics' as we called them? Do you recall the rubbers, the heavy work type and the thinner dressier type? During earlier years we didn't have them but eventually we acquired them and passed them on through the family. The rubbers were to be removed before entering anyone's house. My guess is that is the reason that people began removing shoes when entering homes since it reduced the clean up time, especially during the winter and spring.

Winter also ushered in sliding. We had sleds from before we moved to the city. Mine had Babe Ruth artistically painted on the middle slat and my brother's was Snowbird, a much faster sled according to him. Prior to moving, we'd slide down a path that joined to a dead end street. This street joined a road on a ninety degree curve or T. We'd go straight across the 'T' top and continue to the end. Only one trouble with this scenario. There was a trolley track that came from the wooded area and met at the 'T' and continued along up an incline, parallel to the road. There was a house on each side of the pathway or dead end road, so your vision was limited. Ordinarily we would hear the clanging of the bell, but we were so intent were our endeavor to see who was the fastest we didn't hear the trolley. My brother went under the middle of the trolley and I went under the rear section behind the wheels. The trolley stopped and we continued on home fearful that we had done something wrong. Well, we had, but not intentionally. They told us that the conductor had a heart attack because of us. Anyway, we continued our sliding activities at the river area. There certainly were enough hills and occasionally they'd block off roads for sledding for a few days. I don't know what happened to Snowbird or Babe Ruth.

Probably our younger siblings used them. I do recall sliding down the front lawn once or twice but it was a very short run and steep. Actually, sometimes we'd let the grass grow in the summer if it was very hot, and slide down the sloping yard on pieces of cardboard. It was fast and fun and we often ended up a tumbling mass of bodies if we collided with each other. We also did the same on other slopes where there was tall drying grass that was not mowed. This often ended up with a king of the hill activity.

During the winter we almost always had a wood stove going in the kitchen. It was a combination wood/coal/gas unit and on one of the covers there were three concentric covers. My mother would use this to heat her curling iron when she wanted to 'doll up'.

Before moving to the city she used a kerosene lamp with the glass chimney to heat the iron. Then she would test it on a paper bag or the news print to check the temperature. Later she used the kitchen wood stove by removing the lid and sticking the curling iron into it to bring it to the correct temperature. In both events she inevitably singed her hair but it made her feel better to have curly hair singed all over. She continued to do this for years after she could well afford to go to a hair dresser. The gas stove also served as a heat source. Finally my wife told her that she was singeing her hair and she stopped . . .

Another game that occupied our time and didn't require any special equipment was jackknife. It did require a knife of some sort; however, early on very few of us had a jackknife. Once in awhile it seemed as if one would magically appear and we'd use it for a variety of activities. One activity was to sharpen a short round branch, about four inches long, on both ends so that when it sat on the ground in a horizontal position, there would be about a half inch beneath each point. We'd cut another branch of about the size of a broom handle. This branch was about two and a half to three feet in length and was used as a bat or hitting stick with a tapered tip. If an old broom handle was available, so much the better. A circle was drawn, about two feet in diameter, a center marked by jabbing the stick in and then we'd start the game. Next, the small double pointed 'Peggy' was laid on the ground. One would address the Peggy, striking the pointed end and flipping it up in the air. Then you'd strike it while it was airborne sending it to a distant location. The distance was measured and someone would have to get it back to the circle by tossing it or hitting it with a stick . . . The dangerous part was the chance of someone getting hit by the sharp flying missile. At least, that is what the parents told some of the kids. Therefore, the game had only a few active players.

The other game was baseball or rather jackknife baseball, where you'd open the knife so that one blade, the small one was straight out and the large blade was half way open. The idea was to place the knife so that the large blade was slightly in the ground and the handle was also touching the ground. The small blade was in line with the handle sticking out at a forty-five degree angle. With your index finger you'd place it under the end of the handle that was on the ground and flip it up in the air so that it spun around in mid-air. When it landed depending on which blade went into the dirt or lawn you scored; single, double, triple, home run or out.

A third game we played was flipping the knife with the blades open, from our knees, wrists, or elbow to have it land on that blade in the ground. I think the game was called Mumblety-peg. In the original game of Mumblety-peg, the loser had to pull a peg out of the ground with his teeth! Flipping the knife from a standing position was disastrous for me only once, I never played it again. I tossed the knife from a standing position and it slipped and went into the thigh of my friend. That incident caused me to have a realistic fear as well as a feeling of complete devastation. What would my parents say? The incident passed but I still clearly recall that episode. It taught me to be more forgiving when someone has an accident that obviously causes them anguish. I do not remember the punishment, but I certainly remember the incident. Whenever they wanted to play that game afterward, I did not want to participate.

During our many adventures we realized that we needed to have money for Bugler and soda or the five cent Frisbee pies that were common at various stores as well as to pay for gas for the outboard. Any kind of job was acceptable. We shoveled snow from sidewalks for twenty-five to thirty cents. That was the usual deal. However, occasionally we'd get taken in by someone who would end up giving us only fifteen cents. They would say, something like, "Oh no, you misunderstood I said only fifteen cents." Now thirty and fifteen do NOT sound alike even to a twelve or thirteen year old.

Immediately after 'The Hurricane', we got a job cleaning nuts and bolts and all sorts of auto parts for a store near the old roundhouse. Much of the material was damaged by water so we wiped it down with kerosene. Rather we dunked the parts in kerosene and let them soak before wiping them. What a dirty job They put all the parts back on the shelves after we cleaned them. The job was tedious and not something we enjoyed but I can't recall why. Some of the parts had cosmoline which is a thick gunky preservative. I had to go look up the definition. The dictionary says, petrolatum is a colorless to amber gelatinous semisolid, that I later saw used to preserve gun parts. Now I wish I had paid more attention. It could have been a black market item. Well, I guess not in 1938. Our hands suffered more than anything else but once the job was completed we moved to other types of jobs.

Newspapers had to be delivered to each house on a particular route and my brother purchased a route. I helped him with that. We had over a hundred customers, sometimes as many as a hundred and thirty. Papers sold for two cents. I recall that it went up to a nickel later on. This means he'd get about a penny a week for deliveries. For one hundred twenty five customers, that is seven hundred fifty papers per week! That gave him one dollar twenty five cents per week plus tips. One good thing was that you got to know all the dogs in the neighborhood. The route went from the park up to Sunset Avenue. Saturday was collection day. Some people would leave the money in a cup or glass at a designated location so we would not have to go back to that house a second time on Saturday. Each day we would rise around four-thirty a.m., pick up the papers and start the rounds. We folded the papers into thirds, then into thirds again in order to toss or sail them to the proper place on the porches. Not surprisingly, my brother became a pitcher. On Saturday a second trip was made for collections. This took us until about ten, then we went to the newspaper office to pay the bill. Only a small number of customers paid by leaving money for us. The majority would pay on Saturday. Most were pretty good about it, however, a few would be delinquent. There were ones who said we didn't deliver the paper, so they got a new paper boy. Apparently somebody's kid wanted a paper route so they would take our papers a few days during the week and tell the people that we had quit, thereby signing up a new customer. It was a dirty trick and couldn't be proven no matter how much complaining you did to the management. Eventually, my brother sold his route to a boy named Marvin. Some people have very low standards and encourage the wrong sort of behavior. My brother said the reason he did so well in Civics was because he scanned the papers everyday; something that at this point could soon become a lost art.

The owner of the bowling alley was looking for pin boys. He apparently needed them quickly, so we went to work for Mr. H, a nice man. The training program for setting up pins took only one or two strings and then you were a full timer. We had never even seen a bowling alley before but once you learned the game then you could handle two alleys at once. Then you could make some money. We were able to do the job and get home by nine o'clock. Later, especially on weekends, we'd work till eleven or twelve. We would never get rich, but we could afford the items which we believed were necessary and have some left over to contribute to the family. We'd give it all to the family coffers and they would designate a small amount to us for spending.

At first we worked only after school, then with experience we started the night shifts. We only worked on call during the slack periods. On call meant stopping in to see if you were needed. We got so that we could handle two lanes with ease and my brother handled four lanes on a few occasions. I tried, and did okay, but that only happened when they had special leagues.

Toward the end of our employment there, I could pick up two pins in each hand and tried three on occasion in order to speed up the process, which made the bowlers happy. On occasion we'd step on the pedal that raised the spikes while getting ready to jump over to the other alley and the spikes would go up and knock over pins because a pin might not have been perfectly centered. Picking up the pins would sometimes knock over others so we realized it was better to clear them all off and start again. It was only a few seconds, but that would throw the bowlers off and they'd get impatient.

I forgot to mention this was duck pins. There was one alley that had a faulty pedal that seemed to consistently knock over a few pins unless you centered them perfectly, a problem when you had two alleys to set up.

Usually, the jobs went to the older more experienced employees or the ones in the clique. Yes, there were prejudiced people and if you went to the wrong church or your parents were not part of the societal group, you didn't get the better job or even get considered for the job. Our tenure there was short lived and we never knew exactly why. The older boys were part of a sports program so we only got their jobs when they played a seasonal sport. It seems that it is still the same that persists to this day.

Naturally, mowing lawns was another activity in our repertoire, a monotonous, difficult job for a thirteen year or even a fourteen year old. Many people would call the school for help but always seemed to wait until the grass was five inches high. It was too difficult to mow with an old reel type mower. The mower weighed almost as much as some of the kids pushing it You could only use short pushes and had to do the same place three or four times only moving as much as a foot to a foot and a half per minute. What made it more difficult was that many people had steep front lawns. These tiered lawns were the ones the experienced guys tried to steer clear of, so the real dummies like myself were hired. It would take two to three hours minimum to finish these yards and they were not that large. Don't forget the raking. Bamboo rakes were good, but the iron or steel rakes were a disaster on some lawns as they dug in and hooked the sod no matter how lightly you stroked. When you finished with these there were always tuffs of grass that were standing upright and the owner would want you to re-cut the lawn and make it even. All that for the same money!

With one woman it was a never ending battle and she only wanted to pay thirty five cents. Finally one day I had had enough and left at five without getting paid. Every kid that asked about her decided they could do without such nonsense. Her lawn was about a foot high amid all the nicely manicured lawns. That was the difference about people with and those without money. Those with money seemed to have 'sticky fingers' as my mother would say. They couldn't let go of the cash. I need to be more cautious with that statement. There were a few who were more than generous and because of that you always did an extra amount of work or did something special. I remember our father telling us to instill good work habits, that we should always see how much you could do, not how little you could do, then the rewards would take care of themselves. When you see a need, do something without expecting a reward; don't stand by and watch. Unfortunately many people today are suspicious if you do something extra for them. They think you are looking for something. Or worse, they were brought up not to trust people, so they live in a world full of anxiety and distrust, hence, many are lonely or maybe even depressed. These people seem to live among similar individuals and they seem to age more rapidly.

I recall our father and mother saying something to the effect that someone needs to have her garden weeded, garbage emptied, or needs his wood stacked, so we did it without expecting anything in return. There are times when we would be on our way to play and see a neighbor walking home with two shopping bags. It was almost an automatic reaction to take one of the bags, if not both of them, to relieve him of the load. A mile from the city is a long way when you are carrying two heavy shopping bags. Those people were also the ones who had almost nothing but would try to give you a few pennies or a nickel, when they had nothing to give. They were on relief. They couldn't really afford the bus fare but they still tried to give you something for helping. We never took anything. We'd leave them at the door and run for all we were worth to the game or whatever we were planning to do prior to offering assistance.

On the topic about getting jobs or earning money, I must relay an incident that involved my brother after we had moved to the other side of the river. We were a little older and we were able to get a job occasionally at the golf club caddying. On weekends, especially Saturdays when they were busy or had tournaments, we were needed. My brother managed to get a couple of steady caddying jobs. One of the foursomes had a minister in it. The other three men constantly kidded the minister about his playing and laughed at his attempts and his getting into the rough. On one morning they teed off and I must explain that you could not see the hole from this tee. It was a blind shot. Anyway, the minister teed off and they laughed and joked because it looked like a slice but the landing was not visible. To make a long story longer, the ball appeared to be lost and my brother looked for it with the rest of the crew. Needless to say various comments were made. The ball was found, but no one knew except my brother. He pocketed the ball without anyone knowing, then walked as thought searching over to the hole and slyly dropped the ball. He called to the nearest player and showed him the ball. The player immediately yelled and jumped up claiming a hole in one. An ACE! My brother said it felt so good to have ended the joking and belittling of the man. That joy also got him a better tip. I must ask my brother if he recalls the minister's name.

I saw a friend the other day and let her read some of this manuscript in order to spark her interest in the old neighborhood and see if she could recall some events that might be recorded for posterity. She read it and remembered some of the locations but not what we were doing. Her home overlooked the railroad switch yard, the bridges and tunnel so it was interesting from her stand point as to our antics She wrote, "While I was playing with my dolls on the front porch you were having one adventure after the other. You done good!". Well, I don't know if we'd done good but we did learn a lot and hope we helped others in a way our parents would be proud.

Have you ever lain out and watched the clouds? The changing of the figures that clouds made? Have you ever gone on a walk and arrived at a spot higher than the rest of the area; a grassy knoll with a good view? And just sat down or lay down with your arms and hands under you head and watched the clouds drifting? Did you try to identify the different shapes or faces that appeared to form? Then attempted to create stories to fit the changing scenes, mysterious stories or fantasy stories?. We probably made up stories to fit every dream and the story would go from one person to the next, a sort of adlib or continuous rambling with interruptions when an idea was stimulated by another's thought or description. We probably wrote volumes this way but unfortunately never wrote one down. I was going to invite my grandchildren to a cloud story time and see what developed.

Slater Museum at Norwich Free Academy, where we eventually spent many hours dreaming about getting back again onto the river 'neath the clouds.

Playing cards, pinochle, poker, cribbage, high-low-game also occupied our time at various ages. Our parents loved to play pinochle with my grandfather and uncle. We learned to play by watching and listening. Then cribbage, a game my father thought was necessary for all of us to learn and we did. That occupied many hours in the winter and also on camping trips. Sometimes we played partners. Occasionally there were only three available so 'Pop" brought home a triangular crib board that he had made. Poker and high-low-games we learned from the Woods group. They had a cabin, more like a hut where we were invited. Later we played after work in the school where we worked as janitors usually after noon on Saturday for about an hour.

There were times of sorrow. The death of one of our comrades occurred on the Fourth of July in front our house. It happened across the street, a Fourth of July accident that could have been prevented! If it happened today he could have been saved. One of the boys had some two inch salutes, and was tossing them, but they ignited and blew part of his hand off, plus damaged his face. Home doctoring doesn't pay off.

Rollin Tires appeared for miles sometimes. There was the whacking of steel rims with a piece of board, putting a nail into the end of the board and using it to push the rim along. The nail would inevitably wear out just when you needed it most. We had some sort of game we played snaking around each other in the school yard or field. There was also having the rim continuously move around you while you stood still and changing hands to keep it rolling. Quite an art or skill. I tried to roll one on the railroad tracks but it kept sliding or slipping off and rolling down the ties. It was a complete disaster as it kept bouncing and you'd lose control. I was never that good and if you lost your rim, it was tough to get another. Old tires were much easier to come by. Another activity we tried was to roll down a small slope inside a tire. Not the best thing as you had absolutely no control except to fall over and that was not always pleasant either.

Have you ever tried blowing dandelions that had gone to seed? That white puff ball which was that ping pong ball sized sphere? Then trying to catch the seeds? I see a small seed suspended in the air after blowing a white mini snow storm and watching the seed drift but what seemed to be suspended, always moved away as I reached for it. Of course, some of the kids would say it drifted away because it didn't like me, or I had poison in my fingers. It mystified me. If I grabbed quickly I sometimes caught them, but a normal reach always sent it away. I now know that the air pressure caused by the hand moving toward the seed pushed it away, but at that time all sorts of stories or reasons were conjured up. None of them were too flattering to the person doing the grabbing.

Once in awhile we could buy Dixie cups of ice cream for a nickel, then they increased to seven cents. It was worth it though because you'd get a picture of an actor or actress or even Lassie inside the cover. On the first cup that I had was a picture of the actress Jean Harlow. I didn't know who she was but I kept her picture until it wore out. I was devastated when she died. Some of the other guys had great collections of covers; I remember licking the covers, then peeling off the wax paper protector to examine the photo. We could only afford these occasionally but sometimes we'd get a chance to lick someone else's cover, however, the photo was theirs if they didn't already have it. Also, we always picked up covers if we saw one lying on the ground. Eventually I gave up because most people didn't toss them. It seemed to be a good way to prevent littering.

Another item we enjoyed was double-bubble gum. These had small comic-strip jokes in the wrappers. Too bad I didn't keep a collection of these. They were more interesting to me than the other gums which had cards with photos of baseball players. This became the fad, but I never had a keen interest in those. My brother was the baseball player and he was a pitcher. Once he was hit in the head and spent a few days in bed and I was restricted to sleeping elsewhere. I think it was on the couch. Apparently, he had been at bat and was hit by a wild pitch but they let him go home. He went to work the next day, passed out in the field, and was sent to the hospital and treated, but the cost to him was two hundred fifty dollars. No insurance, so he used his hard earned cash that he had saved for flight lessons in the CAP. (Civil Air Patrol) I knew nothing of this episode until years later when he told me how he had to spend his savings for doctor and hospital bills. Today the school would have paid but not then. Perhaps he would have been a world famous pilot. Who knows?

Today I received some devastating news. My brother was just as shocked as I was when I told him sometimes people could recall earlier times even when their immediate recall was limited. Frannie has Alzheimer in the advanced stages. What a shock to us. We had planned to call on her when he got back up north this year and ride over to our old stomping grounds. Guess we'll do it anyway and try to recall all the things she did that were humorous as sort of a memorial to her. What a shame! Why?

Another activity . . . saving! We saved just about everything that we thought was useful . . . My wife has conniptions with our cellar, but you never know when you might need something. One of the artifacts which we collected was string. Years before the arrival of tape, string was used to tie packages or wrapping paper, so we saved string. Each store had a ball of string in a wrought iron dispenser. Yes, I have one in the cellar where a ball of string was placed and the end hung down to the counter so that the clerk could easily tie up the purchase. We had quite a ball of it, but after we moved it seemed to have disappeared.

One of my final reminiscences is of high school teachers: a Miss Peck, for one. Apparently, I antagonized her and didn't realize it. I didn't know what it was that I would do to set her off but suffice it to say I spent time in the main office, sometime for as long as two weeks at a time. The interesting thing is that my grades always improved when I sat in the office and completed my work. I really liked her, but apparently was the irritant that rubbed her the wrong way. So, Miss Peck, if you ever have the chance to read this, I really am sorry and wish I knew what it was that I did to cause you so much misery. I was even put into the front seat for close observation, however, even that didn't work. You gave me the opportunity to play the part of Nathan Hale and for that I also thank you. Indirectly that instilled the importance of loyalty and integrity because of his willingness to give up his life for his country, thereby setting some of the standards I set for myself. Also, you and my eighth grade teacher, I think it was Miss Clooney, may have set in motion my appreciation for poetry. I still don't care for free verse, and contrary to what others believe, I still think 'IF' is a great poem. Two other teachers I recall who directly influenced me for different reasons were Miss Prior and Miss 'Bette' McMann. Perhaps I showed promise for my teachers and other influential people, considering that they pointed me in the right direction or at least a direction. The Art School, (Miss Cupid, Miss Triplett, Mrs. Browning) was a refuge for many of us and helped offset the need to write. Many of us were allowed to paint posters or make some sort of usable art other than writing. On reflection one person in the art school was a boy named Jack A. who lived in our area. I understand he received a scholarship to some western college and eventually became a teacher. Actually quite a few of us became teachers and returned what we had received. I guess the time has come for some serious thought about those who were successful and contributors from our area. I don't believe that Jack was part of our immediate group of River Rats, but a real nice guy.

I believe there was a young man named Cardoza whom I really liked and who sat behind me and may have been instrumental in helping me make periodic trips to the office. As I mentioned, I almost always got A's and B's while working in the office, so why couldn't I do that in class? Miss Peck was a nice lady, but I had been put in with a crew that may not have been as astute in some ways. The only activity other than playing Nathan Hale that I recall is a poster I made. Sometimes teachers and guidance councilors had no idea of our potential. My brother had a comment written in his record, that said he was definitely NOT college material. He saw this when his record was left on the guidance person's desk and he looked into it. My brother went on to get a Bachelor degree, a Masters, a sixth year certificate and held numerous responsible positions. Definitely NOT college material.

Frank K. told me a similar story of how he was told that he was definitely NOT college material. He held rank in the Air Force and has an engineering degree, BUT was definitely NOT college material. Charlie P. went on to become an inventor, working for the Pentagon, but was definitely NOT college material. He managed to do well as a Physicist/ Engineer. One more story that was mentioned to me by a teacher, Joe T, tells of a student who was a brilliant student but never got involved with various and sundry activities and in his third year applied to five colleges, getting accepted by all, so in his senior year he decided to check with his guidance teacher to be sure he had done everything correctly. He had just receive his signed 'contract' with a prodigious college. The guidance teacher had never seen the boy before and told him there was no way in hell that he could ever get into college. The boy merely reached into his pocket, handed him the acceptance letter and contract and asked, then what does this mean? Needless to say the councilor was speechless. Someone should write about these early school attitudes that were aimed at catering to the upper social group. Some of those people were probably not too bright versus the more intelligent from the other side of the tracks. A detailed article on integrity might be worthwhile but that might cause some eyebrows to lift if it hit the newsstands. I have in mind two men who thought that their integrity was worth more than their jobs. One gave up two lucrative positions because he refused to pass or okay work on a job he thought was unsafe and unethical He had six children at the time. Another was a man who had two years to go until retirement and refused to sign off on a valve that he deemed unsafe. Given the opportunity to sign or leave, he left. He had no pension, no insurance and he lost all. A year or so later the Thresher sank. How do you prove all these things? It is too late now but the truth should come out so that new blood can stand up for what is right. I know that I made it my business over the years to see that the underdog got a fair deal. If I had anything to say, and I did on many occasions, it was at my own expense. My wife still gets angry with me saying they always want me to do the dirty work. At least I can sleep even though most people don't know what I did to help and they most likely will never know that I did help. They thought that I was unresponsive to situations. Not so! Sometimes if you argue with a fool it ends up with the bystanders not knowing who the fool is. They still have to live with their misinterpretations and lies, not me.

# CHAPTER X

## THE LAKE

It occurred to me that some reason should be given as to why we left the river area and became lake dwellers. Tragedy struck and ended our life on the river. Our brother 'Potchie', aka Duane, was accidentally gassed due to the Thermos' heavy demand for gas generated at the G&E in Greenville where our father worked. Had the Thermos not exceeded their need, the pilot light on the hot water heater would not have been extinguished. When the gas reached its normal flow, the pressure prior to the demand, the gas resurged to the houses and unfortunately, there was no pilot light to ignite it and it leaked into the house, killing our brother and almost killing a seventeen year old girl attending him. This was a tragedy with which our mother couldn't cope by living in this house, so we moved and eventually lived in a house build by mom's father. It was where she lived as a girl during her pre-teen and teen years.

Along with the move came a new neighborhood and an invitation to join the Bums, but it sure wasn't the same. We still had the boat and now a car, a 1932 Buick. Pop had friends who owned land and he leased a plot for 100 years and built a cabin on it at Gardener's Lake. Our Hadie Lou II now had a home on a lake so we spent the entire summer living alone. All the other neighboring people living there were guardians and so supervision was more than adequate.

At the lake we worked at neighboring camps doing a variety of jobs from washing dishes to boat handling, and mowing lawns, just general handy-boy stuff. Our cabin was situated on a higher elevation with a path passing other campsites to the spring. One family lived just below us in a squad tent which was WWI vintage. It was not unusual for us, or anyone to pick up an empty water bucket and fill if for them. All water had to be retrieved from the spring down near the lake.

The lake itself was about three and one half miles in length and approximately a mile wide with an island close to our mooring area. Originally, all the land around the lake was owned by four or five families, one of whom Pop knew, hence the lease. There were perhaps eight to ten cottages in the area plus two or three tents, and one family with a gorgeous looking daughter. The family that stands out most in my mind was Mattie's family. Mattie was about our parents age, about five feet one and about one hundred fifteen pounds and as my mother would say, a devil on wheels. She was humorous and kind hearted as well as quite clever in all respects. She had one habit that was memorable. I can't remember seeing her without a cigarette in her mouth. Not only that, it was always in one corner or the other of her mouth. She'd cock her head in order to avoid the smoke getting into her eyes and inevitably had at least a half inch to an inch of ash suspended at the end. This would not have been so bad, but she'd be cooking or something and without fail the ash would eventually fall into the soup, salad, or whatever while she was cooking or preparing.

"Ahh," she said, "it'll add flavor." She was a practical joker and could plan an elaborate scheme at the expense of someone else. There was always a fire going or smoldering in the outside fire ring from the time they set up camp until they closed up for the winter. At night it was the gathering place for many kids and families. There were nights of stories, singing, laughter and occasionally marshmallows. It was a great summer.

The job at one of the camps gave us spending money plus food. We had moved temporarily to a boarding house while the new house Pop bought was vacated. The lake served as a transitional period, adjustment and healing time. We spent two summers there and after we moved to the new home, we'd walk the twelve miles or hitch-hike to the lake on weekends. We always talked about the river as our home.

Mattie and her family lived in an area called the East Side. There was a huge watering trough there for horses. It was constantly fed by spring water. The water would overflow and run down the street to a drain grate and then to the river. People came from miles around to fill their jugs with fresh spring water until the town declared it unsafe.

Although the trough has been disconnected and moved, it was only moved a couple hundred feet and was dedicated just a few years ago as a lasting memorial to the East Side.

The Hadie-Lou II was the queen of the lake for many years. I can't recall when Pop sold the cabin but I wished many times that he had not. I think the last time I was at the lake and in the cabin, it was January while I was home on leave. My companion thought it was nice but never got the true feel for it because it was soooo cold and dank. Had there been heat perhaps we would have made coffee but then the walk to the spring for water would have meant breaking the ice. The car had a heater of sorts but it was cold so we headed back home to the living room.

Memories of the lake show me now how wise my father was to take mom away from the city on weekends and the memories that must have plagued her about the old house near the river.

The lake was normally fairly placid, until the rain and winds came roaring down its length. Then the waves and white caps which were reminiscent of the river beat and crashed on the shore at the casino. The casino meant a dance floor, entertainment area, hot dog, soda, ice cream, hamburger and bait distribution center.

I recall one night when my brother and I headed home going across the lake into a stormy white capped night. We were in the Hadie-Lou II while people on the porch and shore indicated we shouldn't do that. It wasn't safe. Of course, they had no idea of our skill with oars and we promptly waded out with our boat. One held it while the other got in on the oars, started rowing then the other hopped in and laid on the other set of oars. Away we went with a few people cheering us on as we headed for the lee of the island, around it and to our sheltered mooring.

On another occasion, we raced a scull and kept up with him for a while, but he was toying with us. However, he contacted our father to have us stop by his house in order to talk with us. We stopped, with some intimidation. He was a very, very wealthy person but he wasn't home so that was that. Eventually we found out that he had gone to Yale and was on their varsity crew and thought we should pursue that avenue by preparing us to row properly. By the time we found out about that, two years had passed and it was too late for me. I was in the service.

My brother reminded me of the hen house episodes that we experienced. In order to lead into that I need to mention a prior incident that led up to it, because two brothers were sons of the farm owners. There were two farm houses adjacent to one another, the old and the new, with a common drive between them. We rented the old one and part of the rent was paid by working on the farm, haying, milking, feeding the livestock, bringing in the cows at night and letting them out in the morning after milking.

My sister, about two and a half at the time, went into the barn with a new coat and matching hat, to watch my father milk. She stood in the wrong place! The cow lifted its tail and deposited new manure all over her right shoulder. My father stopped milking and took her in to mom, not a pretty sight, but it was humorous at that time.

The owners two sons, one was engaged to be married and the other was a nice looking younger version with blond hair. Bob, by name. Herb brought his fiancée home to meet the family. Big mistake! She fell in love with Bob and eventually married him. I recall them riding side by side in the wagon bringing logs in from the wooded area and I didn't really understand it all until my mother explained it. I do recall Herb not being too happy at the time and, of course, my mother's explanation helped me understand it somewhat. My brother reminded me that Herb eventually became a general and he seemed to think that Bob did also.

Anyway, each year there was a need to clean out the henhouse and sanitize it. That meant cleaning out all the woodchips and shavings with all the manure and what made it worse was that it always was done in the summer! Yes, it smelled pretty ripe. Of course, it was not as ripe as when it sat through the summer in a pile that would be opened in early spring for spreading. That is almost unbelievably rancid. This was hand shoveled to a chute in the waiting wagon and then to the storage pile. Some of it was sold to neighboring farms. After cleaning the henhouse, it would be sprayed with hand pump sprayers and then let sit for awhile. It was then whitewashed. The disinfectant used was to get rid of any vermin and lice, and this included the laying boxes. We had to renew the oyster shells in the yard for the calcium the hens needed for egg production. After that, we waited until night and vaccinated the chickens. It was quite a process. That is why the brothers were there, to help with the vaccinations. This took place long before the river.

By the time we lived at the lake, we were rather accomplished at pinochle and cribbage. Using the glow of kerosene lamps and lanterns we would play till someone fell asleep. We always left a lamp turned down low, a night light in case you had to get up during the night. If we were low on kerosene then there was no lamp. It was not used on moonlit nights. Another reason we used the light was that going to the outhouse at night was hazardous if you couldn't see the trees. We did have flashlights or the lanterns for that. Usually, we used the lantern as the night light, then you could carry it to light your way to the depository. I laugh when I see movies and they are holding the lamp or light up high at face level; no one would do that because the light would blind you. You should use the light above your head or if it was a lantern, at waist level so as to let the light shine in front of you or near your feet so you could see the path and obstacles, but never at face level. Eventually, we bought gas lanterns and lamps. I recall having them when I was very young and learned early on that you didn't touch the mantles. They disintegrated and disappeared as if by magic

Time to close and quote my brother. "Danny, we lived in the best of times and had the best of experiences. What great memories we have. And no one was really poor, we just didn't have any money but we had fun and made our own worlds filled with all kinds of adventures that other kids could only dream about. But the opportunity of poverty and the ingeniousness displayed through creative games we played certainly helped shape our lives and our chances of success and survival without jealousy or resentment for our fellow beings and their triumphs" Brucey, thanks for being my brother, my other self. I only wish you could be here to see the final result of this paper that you helped inspire.

# The Apple Tree

The plan was made, today was the day-
Gas in the tank, oars just in case,
Pick her up at the woolen mill quay,
Then downstream at a Vikings pace.

But she wasn't there for our rendezvous date
The wait was unbearable, so I walked to the hut
There they engaged me in talk, that t'was my fate
Then she appeared in dungarees and shirt-tailed butt

To the boat we did walk, did I hold her hand?
Maybe while I assisted her into the boat,
Strangeness prevailed as we left the land
Sailing along the wharf lined coast.

Then past the break water close to trading cove
A turn to the east through the mud-flat reach
The sun in the southwest, a late august trove,
Past the small island, to the adjacent rocky beach.

Ducked as we came to the over-hanging branches
And lifting them we glided to the gravely shore
Looking up through the boughs and leaves
We saw the top of the old apple tree

So we climbed and sat opposite each other with smiles
And then with courage amassed, I asked with bliss
Holding my breath with fear all the while
She said yes, leaning forward with hands on my face delivered a kiss!

My world was almost complete
I had accomplished an unusual l'amour
Little did I know how innocent the feat
While she, the same age, was much more mature.

The years have progressed at an alarming rate
Fragmentary thoughts have passed through the cells,
Recalling the visions of that infamous date
And wondered, did she kiss and tell??

Next morn I returned to the dock for a swim
The guys all heckled me and called me names
Such as 'kissey kissey on an apple limb'
Henceforth my life would never be the same.

But in my heart there's a place I know
Where there's always a drummers beat,
Plus a light breeze does blow,
And that's in an apple tree of a summer so neat.

# Autumn Serenade

Does music really set your mind
  to a wandering dreamy state?
Does it get right down inside you
  and increase the heartbeat rate?
Is there a whelming of elation
  as you burst forth into song?
Is there a warm and cheery feeling
  in seeing the righting of some wrong?
Oh there's a joyous, religious beaming
  just aching for release,
It's a melodious rapturous reasoning
  to put the world at peace.
And scenes of pastoral splendor
  parade before your eyes
In an endless chromatic rainbow
  as an autumn painter's pride.
You can feel the tune's excitement
  as a September serenade
Passes on into October
  and the leaves reduce their shade;
And the colors all are falling
  in a soft, almost silent sound,
Then a gentle breeze entangles
  the colors on the ground;
Reflecting back the music
  in a scampering, trilling race,
Swelling with shifting colors
  the crescendo now takes place.
Then, a solitary leaf flutters
  from the place where it was hooked,
And lands without a splash
  in the slowly moving brook.
There, resounding with many others
  in a harmonious, colorful ring,
The symphony now starts all over,
  with a whole rest till it's spring.

# An Apple Tree II

Would you like to go with me
To a place that I know-
Where it's always summer
And a light breeze does blow?

In my mind I see it so clear
And so serene-
The setting is rustic,
but also marine.

On the edge of a bank stands
An old apple tree
With branches hanging over
Water that's up to your knees-

A boat sits beneath the 'ore
Hanging boughs
Its empty and lonesome
But that's just for now-

For at the tree-top there
Sits a boy and a girl,
He mustering courage up,
She her hair does twirl-

Finally he asks her,
This cute little miss
If he could have just one,
One little kiss.

For him it was wonderful
To her just a lark,
He was so stupid
She was so smart!

# Low Tide And Barefoot

Ten or eleven, the age to be,
Foot loose and fancy free;
Barefoot at the shore he stands
Squiggling toes into the sand.
Then wading with water to his knees,
Climbed a rock enshrouded in seaweed.
A ballet he then did perform,
As from rock to rock he balanced long.
Squatting, into the deeper water gazed
Into the clear pool he stared amazed!
Heeding not the slippery mess,
Nor the barnacles that tear the flesh;
His soul and soles protectively encased,
Belief in Nature is what a boy's life is laced;
Then from rock to rock he danced again,
Back to shore where his shoes have lain.
Spying a barnacled piling standing free,
A remnant of a dock from a raging sea-
He carefully avoided a sharp shelled path
And ventured to examine the stele shaft,
Where once boats moored near a protective spit,
But in one raging hurricane the piling split.
Partially buried in sand and mud and rock,
Were timbers that once formed a sturdy dock.
An eel, a crab, moved to the marine grass,
Cautiously they moved to the concealing mass.
As he with equally cautioned moves
Investigated the enticing growth in grooves.
Squatting to watch the enthralling plants,
A turbulent rogue wave soaked his once dry pants.
There, a starfish in a feeding mood,
Slowly moved to the mussel food!

He watched the hundreds of feet attack,
The mussel opened to provide a snack.
Then with wet clothes another sight,
On the beach rose hips, a sweet delight.
In his rush to feed he stubbed his toe,
Then stepped on a briar adding to his woe.
But barefoot boys often with this stuff collide,
After a hip or two the pain did subside.
Tough feet are normal for a barefoot boy,
Let nothing deter your low tide joy.

# Green and Grey Monuments

They left their marks in stones of green and grey,
So much beauty attesting to their artistic revelations;
Men who rolled, lifted, stacked each into a place to stay,
Standing as sentinels or guardians for future generations.
A tribute to their enormous endeavors . . .

Who were these men, and women too,
With broken fingernails, knuckles shinned,
And perhaps a crushed toe or two,
Still able to laugh or at least they grinned!
A tribute to their enormous endeavors . . .

They cleared the land of dirt covered boulders,
Deposited by glaciers then thousands years ago,
Gone for hundreds of years, these stalwarts soldiers,
But their monuments remain in an undaunted show!
A tribute to their enormous endeavors . . .

They didn't know they were poor. They didn't know other people were poor. They were taught work ethics and manners. Whatever you do, don't embarrass the family name. These were the facts of life. Family first, chores second. Then freedom to pursue their own adventures. They were trusted, they were appreciative and thankful. Read now and reminisce or travel back to yesteryear.

Central Vermont Engine 220, located in Shelburne Village, Vermont

Edwards Brothers Malloy
Thorofare, NJ  USA
September 17, 2013